A Rose for Raymonde

A Rose for Raymonde

By Wade Foy

ISBN: 978-1-883911-98-0

Brandylane Publishers, Inc.
Richmond, Virginia

19 May 1952

TABLE OF CONTENTS

ACKNOWLEDGEMENTS

This is a good place to emphasize and to acknowledge the tremendous debt my family and I owe to Carl and Lydia Glock of Pittsburgh, PA. They supported the van Laar family in their effort to leave France. They provided encouragement when Charles and Dichette were getting started in the U.S.A., and they gave moral, financial and legal assistance to Dolly and Raymonde in their immigration processes. These friends were truly salt-of-the-earth.

In composing this book I have been greatly assisted by my daughter Virginia Streeter and son W. Charles Foy, who were careful with their reviews and happy with their criticism. It is a pleasure to acknowledge the encouragement given by my daughter-in-law, Maureen Streeter Ross, who reported reading some sections with tears in her eyes.

The support of my publisher, Robert Pruett, has been exemplary. My marvelous editor, Tamurlaine Melby, cannot be praised too highly; to her is due the glow of this finished product.

INTRODUCTION

The 20th Century has seen such a succession of triumphs, depressions, wars, fanaticism, celebrations, mob actions, atrocities and philanthropies that its history would have to be told in many volumes. With such a morass of startling events, one might be tempted to compare a single family's history to an insignificant drop in a vast ocean. On the other hand, this particular story of two lives intertwining may constitute a thread of continuity through this tumultuous century, and its example may offer a measure of hope for a personal good life.

Here, then, I offer the account of a pair of life streams that merged: my own and that of Miss Raymonde van Laar, the beautiful and courageous lady I married, and who is my great true love. These are personal stories, biographies or oral histories if you will, and as such are guided by concerns for family reading. Indeed, much of the original impetus to composition was provided by our daughter Virginia and son Charles. Despite the personal nature of this book I do hope that we have in these accounts enough of novelty, happiness, failure, success, love and the simple truth that derives from a backward gaze to hold the interest of the general reader.

To clear up possible misunderstandings, let me

explain that Raymonde's native language is French; her family immigrated to the U.S. from Switzerland when she was a girl. Among French speakers, it is common to take a male first name and add "e" at the end to make it feminine. Thus, "Raymonde," pronounced with a musical lilt, a slight accent on the "ond" and the "e" silent, is definitively female. The corruptions introduced by people unfamiliar with this French practice have been innumerable, particularly in the U.S.

Raymonde was a Licensed Vocational Nurse and a Registered X-ray Technologist with many years of practice. I have a Doctor of Engineering degree from Johns Hopkins University and have retired from a scientific career in research, development and teaching. We came close to realizing the "married-and-lived-happily" state of the classical romances, though the road we traveled has had its twists and turns. Our times have offered up many trials and catastrophes—the financial crash of 1929 and subsequent depression, World War II, the Korean, Cold and Vietnam wars. As a young woman, Raymonde endured German occupation in France, the trials of immigration to the U.S. and the difficulties of making her way in New York City. I served two years active duty in the U.S. Navy, followed by service in the Naval Reserve. We met in 1951 and married a year later, when she was 29 and I was 27, living out our first year and a half as a "Navy couple." Our life together took us from one end of the country to the other and yielded a lovely daughter and handsome son. The marveling grace is that, except for the Navy tour and voluntary travel, we could always be together, ending the day in each other's arms.

When I undertook the composition of this history, my objective was to capture the memory of Raymonde. The result, of course, was more fruitful still. It is my hope that this book will preserve a glimpse of the world she lived in: her times, her family and the people, places and forces that made up the topography of her life. My daughter and son have been hearty supporters and reviewers throughout this process. Much of the information contained in these pages came from long conversations and story-telling sessions with Raymonde and from many of her casual remarks. I have not been able to review these with other members of her family. I do have passports, immigration documents, letters of recommendation, school reports and resumés for job applications. Raymonde's birth certificate, in Swiss French, is especially interesting. There appear in this book direct copies of several personal letters and notes; in the interests of historical integrity these have remained unedited. Mistakes in grammar, spelling and phraseology often can reveal a lot about a person.

Our story begins in 1951, prior to which I had resided in my parents' home in Richmond, Virginia and in Pollocksville, North Carolina. I had graduated from the U.S. Naval Academy in 1946. Raymonde was born in 1922, grew up in Switzerland, then France, and came to the U.S. with her family in 1947; she took up residence in New York City. There she befriended Mildred and Clay Taylor, the couple who "adopted" me as a lonely student colleague at North Carolina State College. They brought us together.

And so we go forward.

Wade H. Foy Jr.

1

✢

ROMANCE

America's popular memory has glossed the 1950s with a sheen of poodle skirts and ice cream parlors, but the years leading up to 1950 were marked by international unrest and inter-country suspicion. Russia had dropped across Europe an iron curtain that fenced off the Eastern European nations. Then in June of 1950, the communist North Koreans invaded South Korea, and the U.S. intervened with the auspices of the United Nations. The result was a vicious war that ended only with a stalemate in July of 1953.

Still, for many Americans, life progressed as expected, with schooling and work, marriages and births. Following undergraduate studies at Annapolis and active Navy duty, from 1949 to 1951 I was a student at North Carolina State College. It was there that I met fellow student E. Clay Taylor, his wife Mildred and their little daughter Kendall. In the spring of 1951 I was preparing for commencement. At the time I could not yet comprehend my windfall of good fortune in befriending the Taylors, nor know that I was about to meet the woman I would share my life with. This is the beginning of a story of love.

My good friend Clay Taylor and I graduated with Bachelor of Electrical Engineering degrees from

North Carolina State College on 10 June 1951. Clay went to work for International Business Machines in Poughkeepsie, New York; he, Mildred and Kendall settled in a home in Hopewell Junction, Duchess County, NY, just east of the Hudson River.

As for me, I took a job as Junior Engineer for General Electric Co. in Pittsfield, Massachusetts. My assignment was on the 11:00 p.m.–7:00 a.m. shift checking out the electronics of gun director systems for the Navy. The work was routine, following our laboratory exercises at NC State, and was only made exciting whenever a coworker lapsed into inattention and received an electric shock from a 300-volt terminal. These moments, though unpleasant for the recipient, produced much bystander hilarity. Pittsfield is a handsome old town in the western hills of the state, and home of the Tanglewood outdoor music festivals in the summer. I did not see much of the town; any time off from the graveyard shift I spent in a half-asleep daze. Clay did well at IBM; of course, there was a weekend on which a private party Clay and Mid were attending became somewhat unruly and his boss gave him a mild reprimand the following Monday morning (Clay and Mid were not amused).

My time in Pittsfield began on 9 July 1951. In July I was promoted to Lieutenant (junior grade) U.S. Naval Reserve and on 4 September, I received orders to report for active Navy duty, following a physical examination in Boston on 1 October. My supervisor at GE said that they could use industrial priorities to have the orders revoked, but I considered that the country's three-year investment in my USNA education had an overriding claim. Nonetheless, my departure from GE was on

2

good terms.

In the second week of October, Mid and Clay invited me to spend the weekend with them in Hopewell Junction. On Saturday the 13th, I drove there, arriving in the early evening. Mid and Clay were renting or leasing a rural Early American home that had once been a tavern; the base print of the circular bar could still be seen in a corner of the living room, and the place still had many of the early doors and fixtures, though indoor plumbing had been added somewhere along the line. Downstairs it consisted of living room with adjoining guest room and WC (water closet), dining nook and kitchen. Upstairs were two bedrooms, occupied by Mid, Clay and Kendall, and a bathroom. The living room had a large fireplace and chimney. All in all, it was comfortable and livable, with a couple of cats as well.

After a good dinner, I was informed that accommodations would be squeezed; another guest was expected, and my bunk would be a mattress, blanket and pillow on the living room floor in front of the fireplace. At about 8:00 p.m. they put Kendall down, I fixed my mattress and visited the WC, and Mid and Clay went to the train station to meet Miss Raymonde van Laar while I listened out for the little girl.

A little later they returned, having warned Raymonde that I was also visiting. I was half-asleep on my mattress, where I had been joined by one of the cats. Mid and Clay went upstairs. Raymonde came through the living room—I was only aware of a young woman looking down at me with a somewhat disapproving glance—and went into the guest room. I mumbled something like "Hi," rolled over on the mattress and squashed the cat, which squalled in protest. All was quiet for a bit, then we heard a loud "clank–clank;" the door from the living room to the guest room had a large, very old iron key and bolt, and Raymonde had locked it. I felt sheepish. Upstairs Mid and Clay were laughing fit to bust. The rest of the night was peaceful.

Sunday morning we were all rising, putting things to right, getting acquainted. Mid couldn't resist asking Raymonde, "Did you feel safe last night?" to which she responded with a defiant grin.

Here were my first impressions of Miss van Laar: a pretty face, large, bright, hazel eyes and smooth, shining, dark brunette hair with a little wave. She was of medium height, about average weight, with a lovely figure. She was beautiful. I could hardly take my eyes off her. When she smiled at me I felt good all over.

We talked and laughed with Mid and Clay, had breakfast and just enjoyed the company. Being good guests, Raymonde and I washed and dried the dishes. We cooperated readily and were careful not to break anything. There was definite attraction between us. My memory of the rest of the day is mostly a happy blur. At times Clay would tease Raymonde about her French accent, which I thought small of him. Her voice sounded delightful to me.

About the middle of that afternoon it was time to bring our visits to an end. Raymonde needed to catch her train back to New York. As Mid tells it, "We were sitting around and I suggested that Clay take Raymonde to the train station. I was answered by three horrified looks: from Wade (who wanted to take Raymonde), from Raymonde (who wanted Wade to take her) and from Clay (who did not want to go)."

I did drive Raymonde to the station, being as gallant and gentlemanly as I knew how. When I put her on the train she had given me her address, her phone number and her permission to write her. I drove back to Pittsfield in a daze; I knew that meeting Raymonde had been of major importance.

Mid Taylor admitted later that after this weekend she called everybody we all knew and bragged with regard to Raymonde and me that she had "done it!"

Back in Pittsfield I wrote Mid and Clay, thanking them for the weekend visit, and I made arrangements to leave GE and report for Navy duty. A check of my orders confirmed that I was to report to USS *Pursuit* (AGS-17) at Brooklyn Navy Yard, just a subway ride from Raymonde's lodging in Manhattan. The U.S. Navy had done me an enormous favor (probably not intentionally, but I was grateful nevertheless). I wrote Raymonde asking for an evening date in New York.

On 6 November I packed my stuff into my little blue Plymouth sedan, drove to New York, and stopped at the Hotel Lexington. At about 6:00 p.m., Raymonde met me in the lobby (only a little late). She wore a little black dress that fitted closely. She was carefully groomed, dainty, comely, graceful, with style, all woman and gorgeous. We went out dining and dancing at the Hotel Pennsylvania. Tommy Dorsey's orchestra played; we danced easily and well together, especially on slow numbers when I could hold her close. It was a lovely evening.

The next day I drove down to Richmond. I packed up my Navy gear, wrote to Raymonde, told Dad and Mom I had met someone special, then drove back up to Brooklyn, reporting aboard the *Pursuit* on 21

November. The ship was a minesweeper converted to hydrographic survey duty. I relieved Kenneth Phillips as Engineering Officer and worked into my duties fairly quickly. I fit in well with Lt. Ernie Cornwall (Commanding Officer) and Lt. (junior grade) Bob Thomas (Executive Officer)–both good officers and good men–and with two good chief machinist mates. The ship was undergoing repairs in the yard.

On the evenings and weekends when I didn't have duty, I courted Raymonde. We took long walks, sometimes all the way from 113th to 42nd Street, holding hands and talking and smiling at each other. On one such walk she began to limp, without complaining, and I found a blister on one of her toes; we took the subway. We often had dinner together, a leisurely spaghetti dish at Romeo's on 42nd, for example. New York City at this time was not a particularly attractive place. The prospect was generally dingy and grubby and overcast by tall, dark buildings. The winter was cold, with icy winds blowing along the streets. One could find relief from the dreariness at places like Rockefeller Center and Times Square, although anywhere one wanted to go was sure to be clogged by a mob. One walked a lot. The subways were fast, timely, relatively clean and safe; there was little sign of the ugly graffiti and danger of mugging that afflicted the subway system in later years. Driving a car in Manhattan was troublesome at best due to heavy traffic; finding a parking space was always an adventure and sometimes a vain exercise. The general population's attitude towards strangers ranged from amiable to assertive to pushy to discourteous to antagonistic. On the other hand, nice cocktail lounges were readily available, and it was easy to find a good restaurant.

I met Raymonde's friends Madeleine Bennett, a French girl who also came to the U.S. after World War II, and Virginia Adams, a North Carolina lady who was her supervisor in the X-ray department at Memorial Hospital. One evening she took me to a department party: tipsy MDs, some happy technicians, some female attendants who looked askance at Raymonde's non-Yankee escort.

On several occasions I took Raymonde to visit my ship, trying to show off. She wasn't impressed. Brooklyn was even more dingy than Manhattan, and the Navy yard was anything but attractive–dark multi-story buildings, few amenities, large pipes running along the ground, dirty canvas fire hoses laid along the piers, a few trees and dry winter grass. One saw yard workers shambling along, sailors in dungarees or blue uniforms looking lost. Access to the yard was always a problem; the ship's company never did figure out the procedure for getting gate passes, so visitors had to be met at a gate under scrutiny of Marine guards and escorted through the yard maze.

In appearance, the USS *Pursuit* was not much better. The little ship lay alongside a pier with various pipes, hoses and electric lines running here and there. It was difficult to keep her clean with yard work going on. Fortunately, the wardroom where I could entertain Raymonde was usually neat; the furnishings and decorations were purely plain and functional. Dinner service was efficient and the food was usually simple fare. Thanks to Secretary of the Navy Josephus Daniels, who in the 1920s had taken temperance and prohibition seriously, no alcoholic beverages were permitted onboard. It occurred to me that Miss van Laar was being particularly gracious in her visits onboard the *Pursuit*; after all, she could only compare her to the comfortable ocean liner that had brought the van Laar family across the Atlantic.

In our walks around town we recounted much of our histories. She told me of the fears and privations in Bayonne under German occupation during World War II, and of her struggles to learn English and find a decent job in the U.S. I came to respect and admire her for her courage and strength, more than any other person I had known.

The attraction between us grew. On the third or fourth date I called up my courage, took her in my arms and kissed her "good night;" our kiss was warm, sweet, moving and exciting. After more than fifty years the sensation is still vivid. I saw her into the house, and then took the subway back to Brooklyn in a happy daze.

As our dating continued we used the car more. One evening we parked in a spot overlooking the Hudson River and smooched so long we missed dinner. There existed between us more than simple physical attraction (though there was certainly plenty of that). There was also shared fondness, admiration and respect. We were in love, and I told her so.

Please remember that we both were holding full-time jobs: Raymonde as an X-ray technologist and I as a brand new ship's engineering officer. Neither of us had a lot of disposable income. This was no idyllic time; but, she and I took delight in each other's company, getting together whenever possible. It was not puppy love. The attraction, touching, hugging and kissing were powerful.

The afternoon of 2 December was a Sunday off work for both of us. We went walking and happened to stroll, hand in hand, into Central Park. The winter air was chilly, but crisp and pleasant. The trees were bare of leaves and here and there, rocks peeked out of the dry, brown grass. As we walked, gentle snow flurries swirled about us on a light breeze. It was delightful just to be together. At some point she gave me a particularly warm smile and I knew the decision-time was at hand. I held her, backed her against a birch tree and said, "Raymonde darling, I love you most completely. Will you please marry me?" After a moment she smiled and said "Yes!" and I felt a huge throb of happiness–such delight as I had never known. We kissed. We walked across the park to a Ham-an-Egger Restaurant to get out of the cold wind. The rest of the evening is a happy blur; I don't even know how I got back to Brooklyn.

There followed regular dates, discussions of which movie theatre to attend so we could cuddle and smooch in a back row, arrangements to purchase an engagement ring, a monthly allocation of part of my Navy pay to my fiancée. One evening we went to a piano recital by A. Brailovsky at Carnegie Hall; as we ascended in the elevator, arriving at the balcony, the operator announced "Seats for all true music lovers!" Indeed it did seem close to the sky. When it was time to pick up her engagement ring it was snowing; I made the mistake of driving the car into Manhattan, took too long to find a parking place and arrived at the jewelers about forty-five minutes late. Raymonde had waited for me! It looked like true love.

In her visits to my ship Raymonde met most of my

fellow officers around the wardroom dinner table. They were on their good behavior for the most part, exuding professional courtesy. When dealing with the paperwork, I, of course, mentioned our engagement and found that my shipmates definitely approved of Miss van Laar. The next morning the following note appeared on my desk:

CHARGES AND SPECIFICATIONS
3 December 1951

In that Wade Hampton Foy Junior, Lieutenant, junior grade, U.S. Naval Reserve, U.S.S. PURSUIT, on active duty, did, while on authorized leave from U.S.S. PURSUIT, in the City of New York, on or about 2 December 1951, in the presence of the enemy, willfully and intentionally deliver up his right to bachelorhood, which it was his duty to defend, and did cause thereby a most serious and irreparable decline in morale and well-being among his fellow officers and shipmates with but one exception.

R. H. Thomas Lieutenant junior grade
U. S. Navy

As Bob Thomas intended, it never came to judicial action!

The rest of the month went by quickly. At some point we called the van Laars to give them the news. I told Mrs. Van Laar how much I loved her daughter. Raymonde said her mother's first question was "How much does he make a month?" I am reasonably sure that we drove down to Richmond so that Raymonde could meet my parents and we could leave the car with them for safekeeping, as it would be of no use to us in New York. I suppose we took the train back up. When I was with Raymonde I tended to forget about everything else.

At one point I got the idea "Let's get married right away!" I almost had her convinced, but at the last second Raymonde said, "It's too rushy!" So, we gave up that idea, but still had dinner with her brother Tommy, who had come over from Long Island to serve as witness.

We agreed to marry as soon as the *Pursuit* returned from its winter cruise. The ship sailed on 7 January 1952 for a four-month Caribbean cruise to conduct inshore surveys, many of which were concerned with the cable landing sites of a tracking system for Cape Canaveral satellite launches. The work took us to islands like San Salvador, to the Turks and Caicos, and to Samana Bay in Hispaniola. We operated out of Guantanamo Bay Navy Base and San Juan, Puerto Rico.

Raymonde and I wrote each other about every other day; the mail arrived in bunches. If it had not been for our letters, I might have gone out of my mind with the separation from my fiancée. The following are a few of the many letters I sent her during this time apart.

Sunday, January 20

Raymonde, sweetheart,

I am a little more reconciled, after today, to our cruise. Since we have to be parted, and I have to cruise, I'm glad we are down here in the Bahamas.

Today I got to go over to the beach, not once but twice! We talked the Captain into letting us send some recreation parties of the men over to the beach to swim, and play softball, and so on. And since I was doing most of the talking he decided I'd better go along to make sure everything went OK.

It was glorious! We took the boat in as close as we dared; the beaches are full of coral rocks and such. Then we dove off the boat and swam in to shore. The water was cool and wonderful, and so clear that you could see quite a distance when you swam underwater. We ran around the sand, and pitched the softball some, and sunbathed, and generally had a wonderful time. I got back to the ship with wet pants, aching muscles, and a fine start on a sun burn. Boy! Will I be sore tomorrow!

Raymonde, we really must take a cruise down here one of these days. These islands are lovely. The land itself is flat, rocky, and covered with warped half-starved trees and bushes. But the sea! Mama mia! The water is amazing! In the deep areas it is a deep, iridescent, glorious blue—in the shallow spots, a light cool green with dark splashes of coral rocks underneath. The wind is a cool steady breeze that sweeps across a thousand miles of ocean. The sun is a big hot globe hanging in a light blue sky with lots of fleecy little clouds running around. And at sunset it turns into a molten globule of gold that hangs a while on the horizon and then quickly pours itself down out of sight, with the horizon painted in long streaks of red and orange and purple! It is glorious!

In the midst of all I think how much more wonderful it would all be if I were only sharing it with you, my darling. We must cruise this way.

Tomorrow morning, honey, we sail for San Juan

to pick up the first mail for the squadron. It will mean news of you–the first in two weeks! Hooray!
I love you, dearest,
Wade

A more typical note is the following:

March 4
Raymonde, my darling,

There is no news at all today. We think we will go to San Juan for mail the day after tomorrow, but we don't know definitely as yet. If so, it will truly be a blessing; everybody needs a rest, especially me.
What I need is a rest from the Navy. I need to see you, and talk to you, and kiss you, and put my head in your lap, and relax. What a wonderful feeling it would be!
Ah, darlin', you're my oasis in the desert, and I've been thirsty for a long time now.
Angel, I'd give almost anything to be back in New York with you now.
Isn't this coming weekend when you are going to Richmond? Traveling is pretty bad, honey, so be careful. And have a marvelous time, okay? I'll be thinking of you, as always.

Good night, my sweetheart.
Love, for always,
Wade

And also this:

Thursday, March 27

My darling Ray,
Only a month and a half more, angel, and we'll be together again. It will be wonderful.
You are wonderful.
Do you know how much I miss you? It is as though a part of me had been torn away when we parted, and I shall not be whole until we are again together.
Honey, our days together in New York seem now like beautiful dreams–dreams to be remembered for always. And to think that we shall soon be married– that too is like a dream. But it is even more marvelous, because I know the dream will come true.
Oh, sweetheart, to hold you in my arms, to kiss you, to love you–thinking of it is more than I can bear.
If this month and a half will only speed by!

Good night, baby doll,
Your, Wade

Our arrangements for the wedding proceeded with Raymonde doing all the work and me writing every so often that "any way and any plans you want, darling, is fine with me," and arranging for blood tests at strange places like Guantanamo Navy Base. The plans were complicated by the unpredictability of my ship's schedule. We were fairly sure the ship would be in Norfolk in May, but the time it would spend there was hard to determine. We might spend a week or two at dock in New York, and departure in June or July for a northern cruise seemed likely. Wedding dates changed often; location shifted from New York to New

Jersey to Virginia. It was enough to drive Raymonde to distraction. Finally, plans were set:

Monday, May 5

Ray, my dearest,

Holy Hannah! Honey doll, you sure do change around fast! So now the wedding's to be in Richmond. I'm still a little confused, but if that's the way you want it, that's the way it's going to be. Will Mid and Clay, and Tommy and Muriel be able to get to Richmond? I sure hope they can. But you set it up any way you want; all I want is to marry you—I don't much care how or where as long as it's legal and binding and all. I just want you to be happy, darlin'.

The news that your mother might be able to come East for the big event is very good. And I hope that Dolly will be able to come with her. It will be really wonderful to have them with us.

Don't worry about the ship, sweetheart. We are all sure that we'll reach Norfolk by May 15. The trouble is that I'm also sure that I have the duty that night! Que lastima—and damn it!

The ship is in Guantanamo now. We made the mail run again this weekend—it will be the last, so I don't think any more mail will get off until we reach Norfolk. And I know we won't get any more until then. It will be plenty hard to go ten days without hearing from you, Raymonde. Your last letter that came today was dated April 28th.

This cruise is nearly over, thank the Lord! How I have missed you, honey! There have been times when I fully believed the damn cruise would never end, and I

felt like jumping over the side. But it's almost over, and I am practically on the way back to you. Whoopee!
Do you know I love you, mi querida, my beloved?

Always, darling,
Wade

On 16 May 1952, the *Pursuit* returned to port in Norfolk. The first day in port I spent at the Navy base, attending meetings on repairs, facilities and visiting arrangements. The Norfolk Navy Operating Base, incidentally, is the largest naval base in the world; it is organized and beautifully maintained, with many amenities. On the evening of the second day my dad, mom and Raymonde arrived at the dock just after leave was announced. I paraded across the gangway with my gear and a bag full of bottles of rum (one of which had gotten cracked and was leaking), accompanied by a seaman carrying a case of champagne. Big reunion! Raymonde was warm and loving; Dad and Mom looked proud and just a bit amazed.

We all drove back to Richmond and made preparations. On 19 May, Raymonde and I were married in my parents' home, Reverend Maclaren Boyden presiding. Mildred Taylor was the matron of honor, my brother Tom was the best man, and Mrs. Lydia Glock very graciously represented the van Laar family. My mother and father officiated, and Ray's wedding dress was borrowed from sister-in-law Evelyn Foy. Our wedding pictures barely do Raymonde justice, but it was a good event with many of our Richmond family members and friends in attendance.

After the ceremonies, Raymonde and I drove to

Williamsburg, stopping in a small cottage of the Williamsburg Inn. We ordered cold turkey sandwiches for dinner, but left most of it. Both of us were tired, strained and in recovery from all the excitement. Neither of us knew much about honeymooning and we just fumbled a bit before dropping off to sleep. It was the next morning, before breakfast, with kissing and caresses, that we got things lined up right and had our delight of love, each with the other.

Our stay in Williamsburg was a time of learning and loving, supplemented by walks around the colonial buildings, dinner at the Raleigh Tavern, etc. I had worried about having to go back to the ship the third day, but a good friend, Bob Simon, called to say that nothing much was happening aboard and I was not needed. Raymonde and I had a full week for our honeymoon.

2

A YOUNG SWISS LADY'S STORY

Raymonde van Laar was born in Berne on 31 May 1922, "fille legitime" (legitimate daughter) of Charles Jerome van Laar, "agronome" (agriculturist) of Gerzensee, and of Henriette Pauline nee Petitmaitre, his wife. A Swiss "Acte de Naissance" of that time tended to be explicit.

The village of Gerzensee, some nineteen kilometers southeast of Berne, is a picturesque collection of well appointed private dwellings and a couple of inns, all very much in the solid, durable Swiss style. A winding road of about two kilometers leads up the hill from Talgut at the crossing of the Aare River. During the 20s, Charles owned and operated an estate here. He and his wife, nicknamed "Dichette," and family lived in a large, comfortable home that still stands; the household included maids, a cook and a governess for the children. The estate included cattle, pigs, an orchard and pasture and wheat lands. The farm work was done by the Maitre family, who also lived on the estate. Charles was an overly casual gentleman farmer, leaving most of the estate management to his tenant.

When he married in 1917, Charles van Laar was independently wealthy, being the fifth and youngest child of a very successful Hollander. He was healthy, handsome and disposed to enjoy the blessings of unearned income without exerting much effort. He was fluent in French, English, Spanish and German as well as Dutch. He met Dichette in Lausanne. She, Alice and Madeleine were daughters of Elizabeth Barriére Petitmaitre, who owned and operated a pension (some thirty rental rooms with meals and maid service) at Villa Florissant in Ouchy, a suburb of Lausanne located on the shore of Lake Leman; the building is still there. Their father had been stationmaster of la Gare de Lausanne, since retired. Dichette was a strong-willed, pretty young woman; she had traveled in Europe and was fluent in German and English as well as French. Raymonde's maternal grandmother was an efficient, hard-working lady who rather disapproved of Charles' lack of useful employment. "Those who don't work don't eat!" she would sometimes say. It made for some interfamily friction.

The van Laar household at Gerzensee did not run smoothly. When the baby Raymonde was brought home, her sister Dorothy (Dolly), three years older, flew into a tantrum; this set the tone of the two sisters' relationship. Her parents indulged Dolly's eccentricities. Three years later, a son, Tommy, arrived; he became the apple of Charles' and Dichette's eyes. Growing up, Raymonde enjoyed playing with the farm animals—new piglets, calves—and found neat hiding places where she could appreciate the valley and mountain scenery. The view across the valley from the house ended with peaks covered in snow year-round: the Eiger, Monch and Jungfrau of the Bernese Alps. She did not mingle very much with the Maitre family children because they spoke Schweitzer

19

Deutch, a guttural German dialect of which Dichette disapproved strongly; the van Laar household spoke French. A governess was hired in the household for the children's education. Discipline was rather lax: Raymonde remembered hiding up in a tree while the lady called around the grounds trying to get her to class. The family did pay periodic visits to Grandmother Petitmaitre, staying at Villa Florissant. A maid there, Agathe Colliard, especially befriended Raymonde, giving her stale bread to feed the swans of the lake.

In 1929, when Raymonde was seven years old, the U.S. stock market crashed and the Great Depression followed. It had been a long time coming. World War I had brought drastic results; prominent were the wreckage of the monarchies of Austria-Hungary, Russia, Turkey and Germany. In the period around 1920, new governments were created and even new states came into existence. This time of flux was followed by a period of reconstruction and then celebration, the excess of which in 1927 and 1928 became known for jazz music, uninhibited dancing and relaxed social constraints. There was a counter-current in mores that led in the U.S. to an experiment in prohibition. Perhaps in consequence there was an increase in financial activity; stories were told of someone who had bought such-and-such a stock, seen its price triple or more, and sold it, making a "killing." A sort of mass gambling fever drove up prices in the stock markets around the world. The boom burst in 1929 with the collapse of these markets, followed by five years of widespread economic depression.

In Switzerland, with its tradition of financial stability and careful investment, the effects of the

Great Depression were not felt as dramatically as in other countries. Nonetheless, many small businesses and individuals found themselves in financial straits. Charles van Laar, as noted, depended on income from his inheritance. Most of his investments were in Holland, in Royal Dutch Shell for example, and the 1929 Crash hit them hard. When companies' profits changed to losses they declared no dividends. Charles lost most of his investment income. Attempting to recoup, he acted on bad advice and sold stocks at the low market prices; in this way he lost much of his principal wealth. On the estate at Gerzensee the van Laar family had a measure of comfort and financial stability, but little disposable income.

Around 1933, in a move never clearly explained to their children, he and Dichette decided to sell the Gerzensee estate (the buyer was artist painter Hans Zaugg). The loss of the family home distressed Raymonde greatly; she had known happiness there. They then purchased a property named La Cour Planté in Villers-sur-Mer, Normandy, where they could open a private school. This may have been inspired by the fact that Dichette's sister Alice and her husband Max Auckenthaler were operating a successful school in Villars, Switzerland, at the time. Thus, the van Laar family moved to France.

Villers-sur-Mer is a town located on the channel seacoast some 14 kilometers west of Deauville with a view on a clear day of England to the north and the port of Le Havre to the east. It was, and still is, supported mainly by the influx of visitors from Paris and elsewhere in France, many of whom kept vacation homes in the town. La Cour Planté still stands, a large three-story building, three blocks from the beach.

The van Laar school attracted students from England, Germany and America, as well as France. It offered study of the French language, camping, horseback riding (there were stables in town), tennis, dancing and beach sports; during the winter, students were taken to resorts in Switzerland for skiing and snow sports. The van Laar children were expected to mix with the students and assist in their immersion in French.

Of all the children who passed through the school, Raymonde always remembered three girls in particular. Kitty Belle Tibbetts (married Tom Steiger) who attended La Cour Planté from 1937-39, was the daughter of the head of Mercersburg Academy, Pennsylvania, and became a life-long friend. Romola Griswold (married Gordon Brady) was the daughter of Ralph and Dorothy Griswold, he an internationally known landscape architect. Anne Glock (married Raymond Etienne) was the daughter of Carl and Lydia Glock, he a prominent lawyer of Pittsburgh, and she active in the Daughters of the American Revolution.

I have often wondered about the quality of instruction at the van Laars' school. Raymonde learned classical piano and accordion, but, for example, she never learned to hold a tennis racket correctly and she was not a good skier. On the other hand, Anne Glock so improved her conversational French that her parents were always grateful to the van Laars. One activity that Raymonde enjoyed was horseback riding on the beach; her favorite horse was named Whiskey. When the occasion warranted, the van Laars took several girls in formal dress to attend dances in Deauville or Caen (medical students' balls, military balls, etc.). Kitty and

Raymonde especially enjoyed the dancing.

While Dolly and Tommy studied at home, from 1936-1939 Raymonde was a day student at Pensionnat Marie-Joseph, a Catholic girls' school in Trouville that is still in operation. She walked or took the bus depending on the weather. Coming from a Protestant family, she did not mingle well with some of the other students–"Those little bitches would say I was a child of sin." It caused a row at home when the schoolmistress reported to Charles that his daughter had learned the Catechism well. On the other hand, she was a good student; her high mark was 85% in moral philosophy and low was 65% in French composition. Afterwards, from 1939 to 1940, Raymonde attended Ecole Ste. Jeanne d'Arc in Villers-sur-Mer, where she was described as intelligent, conscientious and of a perfect education; she always gave full satisfaction to her professors (these accolades sound much better in French).

The spring of 1939 brought a major turning point for all of Europe. On a visit to Lausanne by Dichette and Raymonde, Aunt Alice told them, "A war is coming, it will be bad. Bring the children and yourselves to Switzerland, and we will help you find a place here." Dichette replied, "We will stay in France to be near by when the old van Laar woman dies." The argument, of course, was that Eugenie de Languedoc van Laar had not lost her fortune in the 30s, and was living in Bayonne. Dichette wanted to make sure that Charles inherited. This course of action was a mistake.

On 1 September 1939, the Germans invaded Poland; World War II had begun. On 10 May 1940, the Germans launched their attack on France via Holland and Belgium. By 16 June the British and some French troops had escaped via Dunkirk and the Germans had overrun the countries down to the France-Spain border. An unoccupied France was set up in the interior with the capital at Vichy. The Germans occupied a zone that extended all along the Channel and Atlantic coasts.

Early in 1940, Charles and Dichette closed the school at Villers-sur-Mer and moved the family to Bayonne on the Atlantic Coast near the Spanish border, to be near Grandmother van Laar. This was a time of misery, privation and danger in most of Europe. Much of France languished under German occupation; in Bayonne the Wehrmacht was on relatively good behavior, but the Schutzstaffel was menacing. There were drafts of people who were sent to forced labor in German war industries. There were conscriptions of Jews—men, women and children—who were taken away to concentration camps. Such actions, after a while, were extended to involve anyone who the Germans thought to be opposed to the occupation. Fear was everywhere. On several occasions Raymonde knew of people who were there one day and with no notice had simply disappeared the next. Like many of the townspeople, Charles, Dichette and family mostly kept to themselves, though, they did make periodic visits to Grandmother van Laar. They avoided doing anything that might provoke the occupation forces. It was only at the end of the war that the facts of Jewish extermination in places like Auschwitz, the starving to death of workers in the forced-labor camps and the failure of French prisoners-of-war to return home became known.

Food was scarce and strictly rationed. Raymonde remembers standing in line in the cold of winter, before dawn, waiting to get a couple of kilograms of fish for a meal. Sometimes Dichette sent her on her bicycle into the countryside to local farms to barter linens and clothes for fresh vegetables or a jar of bacon drippings. Fuel was also short; on some winter days, the van Laars had to cover themselves with bedding just to stay warm.

Charles took a job with the Bayonne town authorities as a translator of German. The van Laar family relations with the townspeople were often unpleasant; they were Dutch and therefore were perceived as "foreigners who took bread out of the mouths of good Frenchmen." They were not trusted to have any connection with resistance activities. It was particularly nerve-wracking that the Gestapo happened to take up residence in a house next door to the family's cottage. The van Laars lived in fear much of the time, and Charles only aggravated family tensions by surreptitiously listening to the British Broadcasting Corporation radio. The German occupation forces ruled strictly against listening to any broadcasts except those they authorized. Penalties ranged from denial of food ration cards to deportation to a concentration camp.

From 1940 to 1941, Raymonde studied at the College Moderne de Jeunes Filles in Bayonne. In July 1942, she and Dolly took certificates of the French Red Cross for medico-social aid. Part of their training was providing nursing assistance to a local peasant family; living conditions there were unsanitary to say the least. Early the next year, Raymonde studied Declamation and Dramatic Art at Ecole Nationale de Music, Bayonne. Then, from 1943 to 1944, she and Dolly practiced nursing on the surgical floor of a hospital in Tours in unoccupied France. This was a time when Allied air forces ranged widely over France, bombing transportation nodes, disrupting traffic and attacking industrial plants. Raymonde remembers being on a street in Tours when an Allied fighter flew overhead; the pilot made a strafing pass just at her, which she escaped by jumping into a doorway.

In June 1944, the British, Canadians and Americans invaded Normandy, and the German occupation began to fall apart. In the chaos and disruption of hospital activities, Dolly and Raymonde left Tours to return to their mother and father in Bayonne. The best transportation they could get was on railroad cattle cars. Twice their train was sabotaged by the French Resistance; once they found themselves on a railroad embankment waiting for a crew to put a flat car back on the tracks. Fortunately they were among the uninjured. Such actions, and the slowness of the trains, made for a harrowing journey and a much-delayed arrival at home.

When the Germans were finally chased out of France, the country was a mess; Gaullists, resistance fighters, Vichyites and others struggled for power. In particular, the Communists seized the time to take revenge on actual or potential opponents, using accusations of collaboration to denounce military families, anyone who owned property, anyone who happened to have survived with some assets, etc. Because of Charles' work translating German and the fact that Raymonde and Dolly volunteered in a hospital that treated German soldiers, the van Laars were accused of collaboration with the Germans. They were hauled before kangaroo courts and sent to detention in a fenced camp guarded by Senegalese soldiers. Only young Tommy, to whom Grandmother van Laar managed to extend her protection, was permitted to stay behind in her keep.

The others remained in the camp for about a year. Though the experience wasn't a pleasant one, and Raymonde spoke of it little, she always said she didn't mind being interned too much, since she was alongside WWI veterans, aristocrats and highly educated people whom the communists viewed as a threat to their influence. She recalled meeting social peers, making friends such as Madeleine Colas and learning to play bridge. Before the year was out, the injustice of their detention became known. Their friend Carl Glock, in particular, was outraged and took steps to bring their case to public notice. With the help of his influence, they were released.

About then Grandmother van Laar died. Through the last year of her illness, she had been nursed by the daughter of Greta, Charles' sister, who also lived in Bayonne; the daughter inherited most of the estate. Charles and Dichette's hopes of fortune were dashed.

While pondering what to do next, they went to live at Villa Florrisant with Aunt Madeleine, who had become manager of the pension when Grandmother Petitmaitre died. Because the van Laars were visitors, and due to some intra-family antipathy, relations during their stay were not always pleasant. Raymonde asserted her independence, answered a newspaper advertisement and, rather to her aunt's surprise, got a job as resident nurse in a tuberculosis clinic in Leysin, a town in the mountains above the valley of the Rhone. She did well and became staff nurse at Clinic Beau-Soleil, earning the praise of Dr. Chaghagi, the head physician. The clinic was a facility of the Swiss Army Health Service, with military and prisoner-of-war patients from France, Belgium, Greece, Italy and Yugoslavia. Her work there lasted until August 1946 when, under protest from Raymonde, her parents took the family to America.

Charles' and Dichette's decision to go to "les Etats Unis" was never explained to their family. I am sure that they had little idea at the time of what the ramifications of the move would be. Even stranger than the enigmatic nature of their decision was their failure to prepare their children for a move to a new country; Raymonde, for example, had not been taught English. Charles and the children, and presumably Dichette also, traveled with Dutch passports. Their assets consisted of little more than La Cour Planté property, which they sold.

In June of 1947 Charles, Dichette, Dolly, Raymonde and Tommy traveled aboard M.S. *Veendam*, Holland-America Line. An incident aboard the ship illuminates the tension that existed between Raymonde and her parents. Raymonde met three elderly English gentlemen who asked her to make a fourth at bridge. This was a pleasant way to pass the voyage time. One evening as they played, Dichette came to the table and told Raymonde to go to bed. She replied, "Mother, I am playing three no-trump!" Dichette left in a huff. When finished playing, Raymonde went to her cabin and found her father in a rage at the "insult to her mother." He reprimanded and slapped her, giving no credit to her explanations. Raymonde lost a lot of respect for her parents that day.

After a ten-day voyage, the ship arrived in New York. The family took up residence in Staten Island, in New York harbor. Upon their entrance to the U.S. there were complications. Because the Dutch immigration quota to the U.S. was filled, they could enter only with visitors' visas. Charles and Dichette, being teachers, and Tommy, being a student, could come in by special exemptions. Things looked bad until, with the help of Carl Glock, Dolly and Raymonde found that because of their father's birthplace they were considered Dutch in Europe, but because of their own birthplace they were considered Swiss in the U.S. The Swiss quota, naturally, was wide open.

There ensued something of a legal farce. In July, Dolly and Raymonde went to Niagara Falls, Canada, taking temporary jobs as graduate nurses at Niagara Falls General Hospital. They returned to the U.S. two months later, "cleansed," as Swiss citizens on immigration visas. The Glocks undertook sponsorship for Dolly and Raymonde's immigration, an action not only very generous, but also involving acceptance of considerable responsibility.

Returning with Dolly to the family in Staten Island, Raymonde sought a job in nursing. Unhappily, her credentials and references from France and Switzerland were not recognized in the U.S. and, with her unfamiliarity with English, the only work she could find was as a nursing assistant at the French Hospital in New York City. This job she endured from September 1947 to January 1949.

In January 1948, Raymonde left Staten Island and took residence at Jeanne d'Arc Home in Manhattan. Her roommate was a young French lady, Madeleine Bennett (married J. Cibil), who became a life-long friend. The two girls took considerable pleasure in agitating the staid, elderly nuns who ran Jeanne d'Arc

Home. Raymonde undertook evening classes in English. She always remembered the good instructor and the problems she had getting her students to pronounce "th" and other weird sounds. Raymonde became fluent, assisted by going to cowboy movies; she said that the first phrase she learned was "He went thataway."

By January 1949, her situation had improved enough for her to get a job as a practical nurse in the X-ray department of Memorial (now Sloan-Kettering) Hospital in Manhattan. There, the department was run by Virginia Adams (married Stanley Lambe). Virginia and Raymonde struck up a friendship there that continued throughout their lives. The chief radiologist was Dr. R. Sherman, for whose professional competence and sense of justice Raymonde developed tremendous respect. In February, Raymonde completed an X-ray technical course at Manhattan Medical Assistants night school. She learned about the positioning of patients for various views, the control of the X-ray machines, the adjustment of radiation intensity, and the development of photographic films. With this training she earned a corresponding job as X-ray technician at Memorial Hospital.

It was during this time in 1949 that Charles, Dichette and Dolly moved to Santa Barbara, California for Charles to take a teaching job. That Raymonde chose not to move with them was a decision that, in retrospect, we recognized as a major turning point in our lives.

Thus, after about two years in the U.S., the van Laar family was split: Tommy in college on Long Island, Raymonde in New York City, and the rest in California. After graduation, Tommy established a landscaping business and married Muriel Harrell, an attractive

Georgia lady. By this time, Charles and Dichette had already spent the profit from the sale of La Cour Planté on living expenses. He now taught French in private schools. Carl and Lydia Glock had expected that the van Laars would open a school in the U.S. like that in Villers-sur-Mer, confident that it would be successful; they offered help in getting one started. Dichette said, "No. I don't want to work." Indeed, it seems she expected her two daughters to marry into wealth and put the family on Easy Street. As it happened, over the years she became obsessed with the fact that Charles' income failed to provide the class of living she wanted, and at various times tried get-rich-quick schemes in real estate and other ventures. A move during this period to Pasadena alleviated some of the family's financial strain but did not eradicate it.

In New York, Raymonde was not entirely alone; during much of her time there, she had good friends nearby. In addition, her uncle Adrian van Laar had come to the U.S. in the 30s and lived in New York as a salesman for Medaglia d'Oro coffee. He took Raymonde on visits to friends on some weekends, and did a bit to show her around. A cousin, Violette Draper-Dobie, lived in Canada not far away and had loaned the van Laar family her vacation place on Muskoka Lake. Still, Raymonde was on her own to support herself, and even periodically dealt with requests for money from her parents in California. Life in the big city had its ups and downs. There were weeks when the money did not stretch far enough, and a lettuce sandwich had to make a meal. In a couple of years she saved enough to travel from New York to Los Angeles by chair car on the El Capitan train in order to visit her parents. She was courted in New York by a well-to-do older gentleman, Galen Halshu, who wanted to marry her, but she did not love him. Dichette, across the country, was in favor of the marriage. Galen took a trip to the West Coast, visited the van Laars, and made the mistake of asking Raymonde's parents to bring pressure on her to accept him. This got back to Raymonde, and she didn't see him again.

Raymonde undertook in 1950 an evening course in X-ray theory and technique at New York University, completing it at the end of the fall term of 1951. Her work at Memorial Hospital continued to be challenging and successful. An incident occurred at the hospital that illustrates some of the difficulties young women dealt with in the workplace at this time. One day Raymonde was in the X-ray dark room developing film when an intern M.D. opened the door and looked in. She asked why he had done so, and he replied, "I wanted to see you with your pants down." She went directly to Dr. Sherman and reported the incident. He called the offender to his office; the intern left and was seen there no more. When it was needed to right a wrong, Raymonde always believed in overkill.

During January 1951, she moved to a rented room in a house on 113th street belonging to a woman named Mrs. Olson. In September she took a break from the hospital, working as a hostess in a Stauffer's Restaurant. It was strenuous. She returned to X-ray work at Memorial in November, holding her job there until September of 1952.

Raymonde had met, via mutual friends, Lt. Col. and Mrs. F. W. Kendall, who were stationed on Governor's Island, an Army base in those days. The island is located in New York harbor about a mile off the southern tip of Manhattan. The view is spectacular, especially when the sun goes down and the lights appear in the large downtown buildings. The Kendalls' daughter was Mildred Taylor, whose husband Clay was a classmate of mine at North Carolina State College. The Taylors' first daughter was Nan, a beautiful child who never developed mentally and was in an institution in New York. Raymonde visited Nan and did what she could to help her. Clay and Mid were grateful and admiring; they were close friends of Raymonde's from then on.

In December 1951, Raymonde and I met, bringing together the two main streams of our story.

3

✿

THE SECOND STREAM

The state of North Carolina is sometimes described as a "valley of normalcy" between two "mountains of vanity" (South Carolina and Virginia). Jones County, in the east, is a country of farms and large estates. The land is sandy, often hot in the summer and chilly with some rain and snow in the winter. Pine forests alternate with open fields. Drought is always a danger. In the late 1890s the cash crop was tobacco, strictly regulated by the government; staple crops were corn, peanuts and soybeans. The river Trent flows by the small town of Pollocksville, where it intersects U.S. Route 17. It was here that Wade Hampton Foy was born in 1885. He went to the rural schools, picked tobacco, sprayed insecticide on growing plants and generally lived the hard life typical of a farm boy growing up with few amenities. By some process never explained to his children, in his early twenties he decided to leave the farm and take up medicine. After rudimentary high schooling, he trekked to Richmond, Virginia, where he studied pharmacy at the Medical College of Virginia, supporting himself with part-time work in drug stores. After taking his degree, he saved enough to open his own Foy's Pharmacy on the first floor of the Shenandoah Apartments, located at the intersection of

Grace and Allen Streets in Richmond. He met, courted and married Eliza Belle Wilkinson of Richmond (born 1896). Eliza was a pretty lady, educated at Stuart Hall in Virginia, with a cultivated singing voice. She was firmly grounded in mid-Victorian principals and beliefs. The couple took residence in the Wilkinson home at 3605 Chamberlayne Avenue.

Support for the family came from Pharmacy profits, with Wade working ten-hour days and Eliza keeping the books. Wade also found time to serve as deacon for St. Mark's Episcopal Church and to take an active part as a member of the Masonic Lodge.

On 26 January 1925, their first son was born. I was named Wade Hampton Foy Jr., and two years later my brother, Thomas Franklin Foy arrived. Growing up, I went through the usual childhood diseases, plus bouts of scarlet fever, mastoiditis and appendicitis. I was nursed and home-schooled at times by my mother. The mastoid case, which struck me at age nine, was difficult, requiring hospitalization and two operations by Dr. B.R. Wellford, a local specialist recommended by the family physician, Dr. W. Blanton.

Tom and I grew up, fought and played, often with our neighbor, Jimmy Taylor, with whom we forged a friendship that lasted well beyond child-hood. It was during our grade school years that a distant relative, Mary Ellen Trimmer, came to live with the family while she attended Richmond Professional Institute. Thus, we boys had a big sister. Whenever Mary Ellen brought her school friends home to dinner, the girls would tell jokes that would set Tom and me to giggling uncontrollably, somewhat to our mother's dismay.

The Great Depression hit when I was five years

old. Businesses closed; storefronts were boarded up; the downtown districts of many cities became almost unpeopled. In the U.S. the unemployment rate exceeded twenty percent, and there were long lines of applicants for any job offering. Charities that put out food had "breadlines" form. Drifting men hitchhiked along the highways. Many families lost their homes and assembled in informal shantytowns, living only on government dole. Some relief was brought by new state and federal governments in 1933, but the U.S. did not fully recover financial health until the industrial buildup to World War II. Foy's Pharmacy survived, in part because a local pharmacy wholesale house extended credit on my father's reputation. The Foy family had consistently operated with careful money management. Now we became more frugal and avoided luxuries such as summer vacations at a rented cottage on the Potomac River. I always remembered receiving a letter with the notice that American Bank had failed and my $100 account no longer existed; all I got, some years later, was a $10 refund. Such an experience led me to an ultraconservative financial policy ever after.

By the mid 1930s, the U.S. hadn't fully recovered from the Depression, but circumstances had begun to ease up a little. Around the time I entered high school, the family acquired a 1929 Model A Ford Coupe. Tom and I undertook to replace its piston rings and timing gear, with barely adequate tools, and the car actually survived. We learned to drive by running the car around the driveway. This car was fun. With all its controls at their limits it could get up to 60 miles per hour, and that felt like flying. By 1941, my final year of high school, I had my driver's license and we sometimes drove the

Model A to school, returning home with four kids in the front seat, three in the rumble seat, and one standing on each side running board, holding on for dear life.

Another project Tom and I took on was the construction of a wooden sailboat, sloop-rigged, that we sailed during family vacations to the shores of the Potomac River and the Chesapeake Bay. The little boat, about 13 feet long and christened "Moonbeam," sailed fairly well but had the bad habit of leaking so much it filled with water overnight: poor design, faulty construction, or both.

Through all my schooling, my ambition was to be a Naval officer. My courses followed a college preparatory program that included Latin. I had a good memory, so Plane Geometry was an exciting challenge. I was a poor athlete. My worst course was Typing—the teacher passed me with a D only on my promise to not appear in her class again.

While I saw to my education, the situation in Europe and Asia was devolving into crisis. During the years from 1935 to 1941, the Germans under Adolf Hitler overran most of Europe. The British held out. The Japanese invaded China. The U.S. news and entertainment industries were riddled with alarm and apprehension. Propaganda was ubiquitous and blatant for all sides. Because of reported atrocities, there developed in the U.S. a widespread fear of Nazi Germany's military and a detestation of Japan's forces. I remember in school doodling pictures of fighter airplanes in action; they were always U.S. versus the Japanese.

On 7 December 1941, I was in my high school classroom when the news came that Japanese planes had attacked Pearl Harbor in Hawaii, inflicting great damage on U.S. Navy ships and U.S. Army bases. It came as a shock to all of us, though the nature of the enemy was not unexpected. We realized immediately that the war had come to us; yet, none of us had a good idea of what that would mean to us as individuals. The U.S. military draft was in effect and all we able-bodied young men went to register; some hardy souls volunteered. I do not recall any fear that the U.S. might lose.

I had a military deferment because of schooling. After I graduated high school in June of 1942, my parents sent me to Randles Preparatory School in Washington, D.C. for a ten-month term, the plain purpose of which was preparation for U.S. Academy entrance examinations. During that term I won a competitive examination for Congressman Dave Satterfield's appointment to Annapolis. In spring of 1943 I passed the entrance tests: three days, a three-hour test each morning and afternoon, Algebra, Geometry, English literature and composition, American History, Physics, Chemistry. All were essays or written problems, no "multiple-choice." In June I went to Annapolis, barely passed the physical examination and was enlisted as a "Plebe" midshipman in the U.S. Naval Academy.

My time at the Naval Academy marked the start of my adult life, and in the meantime, others were building lives of their own. After high school, my brother Tom enrolled in a Navy V-12 program at Duke University. He went on to earn his BS degree, work in Richmond for a while and marry Evelyn Eades, a lovely lady. He continued on to the University of Michigan, took an

MS in Mechanical Engineering and went to work for General Electric Co. in Massachusetts. As for Jim Taylor, he went to Virginia Military Institute, graduated and built a very successful career in chemical products and the petroleum industry. He married Jeanne Ancarrow, who is a great lady and a good friend. Mary Ellen earned her bachelor's degree and undertook social work in Richmond (the boys used to tease her about being a "truant officer" for South Richmond schools). At a University of Richmond affair, she met physics professor Jackson Taylor. They married and made a home near the University and Jack turned out to be a life-long friend. My cousin Eddie Foy settled in Richmond and married Martha Darden, who became a pillar of the family.

At the Naval Academy I was fortunate to be in the same company as J. Douglas Rumble, who had been a day student at Randles; Doug's father was an active duty Navy officer. We roomed together the full three years at Annapolis, and no one ever had a better friend than Doug. Plebe year was full of the usual drill. Under Marine instructors I shot well enough on the ranges to earn Expert Rifle and Expert Pistol qualifications.

In academic studies I did well; my good memory was a major benefit. The quality of instruction varied from good to miserable. In athletics I did poorly; at the September start of each class year I would flunk, requiring practice runs each weekday afternoon until I could get my time on the obstacle course below the required level. The excellent physical education program at USNA made a big improvement in my strength and health.

During my Naval Academy years my "steady date"

was Katharine Hunt–bright, brunette, shapely, very pretty–whom I knew from high school and Miss Julia M. Harper's Saturday evening dancing cotillions in Richmond. Kitty would come to Annapolis for a weekend of sailing, watching the midshipmen parade, and dancing at a Saturday evening ball ("hop" in USNA slang). At the time midshipmen were not allowed off base except for some Saturday afternoons and evenings. On the weekends when there were dances, the girls would arrive on Saturday morning and the midshipmen had to make arrangements for them to stay at one of the many houses in town that had made a business of letting out rooms for these occasions. We would dance the evening away, and right at the last note of the last song the duty officer would set his stopwatch, and the lower classmen had exactly 45 minutes to get the girls off to their rooms. The townspeople of Annapolis would often stay up late on Saturday nights just to watch the surge of midshipmen charging back to the front door of the dormitory in a mad race to get in by curfew.

Upon graduation in June 1946, Doug and I were commissioned as Ensigns, U.S. Navy. Doug went to duty on a cruiser. I had three changes of orders before being sent to the newly commissioned USS *Henley* (DD762), a destroyer, in San Francisco. Kitty Hunt and I wrote back and forth a few times but gradually lost contact. She went on to marry a long-time boyfriend, and they settled in Richmond.

The *Henley*, Commander D. L. Moody commanding, went from San Francisco to shakedown in San Diego, back to repair at Mare Island in San Francisco Bay, then along the west coast of Central America, through the Panama Canal, to six months duty as station ship for the Navy Sonar School at Key West. This was followed by a voyage to Gibraltar and a showing-the-flag tour of the Mediterranean, operating with an aircraft carrier and another destroyer. We visited France, northern Africa, Malta, Greece, Turkey and Italy. In the winter of 1948 we came back across the North Atlantic with storms all the way to Boston.

For my duty aboard the destroyer I was at various times an excellent anti-submarine-warfare officer, a fairly good torpedo officer, a fairly good assistant gunnery officer, a fairly good assistant engineering officer, a fairly good officer-of-the-deck underway, a good navigator and a poor wardroom mess treasurer. This all produced unsatisfactory marks on two fitness reports, which, of course, doomed any chance I had of a successful career as a U.S. Navy officer.

In February 1948 I submitted my resignation as a regular U.S. Navy officer, which was a great disappointment to my father, my mother and my congressman. I was offered comparable rank in the Reserve, accepted and was commissioned Ensign, U.S. Naval Reserve, going on inactive duty in October 1948.

There followed a blue period of uncertainty in which I worked odd jobs, contemplated my sins and questioned my future. I decided to take up electrical engineering and applied for admission to North Carolina State College, which had a good reputation for studies in automatic control systems, a major interest of mine. In September 1949 I entered NC State as a junior. I had a BS degree from the USNA, but the electrical engineering courses were rigidly sequenced. I even had to take the last quarter of sophomore chemistry.

Once at NC State I began to find some sense, feel more purposeful and apply myself to something useful. I did well in my studies. The instructors were good, especially the Electrical Engineering Department Head, Dr. Brennecke, who taught the mathematical analysis of transients in systems, a basis for control systems studies. Many of my fellow students were military veterans being supported by the GI Bill. I got along well with them.

More importantly, my first laboratory partner was E. Clay Taylor, who had fought in the War. We managed to burn up some circuits together and became good friends. Clay, his wife Mildred and their little girl Kendall were living in married students' quarters near the NC State campus. Mid would invite me up for spaghetti dinners, and I would baby-sit Kendall on occasion. It was a time of low income, hard studies, long written laboratory reports and good classmates. I even found the confidence to date some nice girls. I was working hard at things I understood, and I liked it. I was given the responsibility of monitoring a floor in a freshman dormitory. Just next door to me in the dorm lived another monitor, Glenn Hardesty, a student of agriculture. He and I struck up a long friendship. I often wonder just how much of a "good influence" we were on the unruly freshmen.

During this time Mid Taylor happened to mention to me a young lady friend of theirs, Raymonde van Laar, who lived in New York. She wrote to invite her for a weekend in Raleigh, to visit and meet me. Raymonde wrote back that she was busy and anyway did not need any more boyfriends. But her name resonated in my mind.

4

1952 – 1955
EARLY MARRIED LIFE

Our short, happy honeymoon came to an end on 24 May 1952, when the *Pursuit* sailed from Norfolk to Brooklyn. Raymonde followed and, in New York, again took up her work at the Memorial Cancer Center X-ray Department. In the Brooklyn Navy Yard, the *Pursuit* was being prepared for work in northern waters. There were the usual annoyances about visitors' access and yard work delays.

In order to be together, Raymonde and I took a room at the St. George Hotel in Brooklyn–an old but reasonably comfortable hostelry in a fairly quiet area. Here we began to take up normal married life: quick breakfast, off to work, happy reunion and loving in the afternoon, quick dinner, loving in the evening. It was marvelous for both of us to have each other's company, even though there were interruptions for shipboard duty. This was a time of melding and great affection. We became a couple, in the best sense of the word.

On 16 June the *Pursuit* sailed, my having been promoted to Lieutenant USNR. This cruise took us to Baffin Bay and the west coast of Greenland; we crossed the Arctic Circle on 19 August. This trip was quite eventful. One report, for example, was the following:

Friday, June 27

Ray, my dearest,
Here it is almost the end of June! And next comes July! And maybe then we'll begin to feel as though this cruise may end before we all go crazy. But the time at last has begun to go by–last week seemed much shorter than the one before, which was an eternity.

Oh, darling, it will be good to get back to you! And the sooner the better! For a while the other night we all thought we'd get back home sooner than anyone had expected–back to drydock, that is. We were in the edge of an ice pack when a storm came up. It was night–cold and wet–with the wind blowing a gale. The waves were getting bigger all the time, and they started dashing big chunks of floating ice against our sides. We were lucky and got out before any serious damage was done, but everyone was mighty glad to finally get into open water. These ice fields are plenty dangerous; we are gonna try to stay out of 'em from now on.

We expect to get to the harbor where the survey work is to be done tonight. It will be a comfort, in a way, to start on the work–I'd hate to think that all this strain of being away from you went for nothing.

How I do miss you, honey doll! To think that, after finding and marrying the girl I've dreamed about for all these years, I had to go out on a cruise after only one month! I should be shot–I do mentally kick myself in the fanny every time I think of it, sweet. But this I swear, Ray my darling wife: I'll come back as soon as I can, and I'll love you even more when I return than when we were in New York–if that be possible.

Good night, cherie,
Your, Wade

When operating in Hopedale Harbor, on July 9, the *Pursuit* ran aground on an uncharted rock. I wrote:

Thursday, July 10

My dearest,
The greatest joy I have, now when I'm away, is to be able to write you and call you things like "my darling" and "my dearest" and "ma cherie." They sound so good and right; they make me feel tingly all over. What I'm trying to say, Ray darlin', is that I'm in love with my wife!

All I know about it is that I'm sick and tired of this Labrador place, and I want to go home to my wife!

We've had two days of the most beautiful weather you ever saw. Bright sun, warm breezes, and a practically cloudless sky–the temperature was up to 80deg this afternoon. I can imagine the terrific heat you must be having in New York.

Ever since last Saturday we have tied up alongside a small repair ship. We have four or five small leaks in our bottom, and the repair ship's men have been trying to patch 'em up. So far they haven't done much good. None of the leaks are bad enough to cause any too much trouble, except one tiny one in a lubricating oil tank. If this one isn't fixed, we will get salt water in our lube oil and probably get some machinery so messed up that we won't be able to use one propeller, which will not be good. However, the repair men are working on it now, and they expect to have it all fixed up before tomorrow morning. I hope so.

I've been keeping slim by crawling around in tanks that are about three feet high. Can you imagine?

There's one thing I know of that Labrador can lay claim to. That is having the biggest mosquitoes in the world. I'll swear, darling, these things that fly around here are not bugs, they're animals. I've seen some nearly half an inch long with a stinger that could reach bone in you. They're monstrous.

I'll be glad when we leave this place. And I'll be hysterically happy when we finally turn around and head for home. I can only tell you that I love you until then, doll, but after—I'll prove it to you!

All my love, angel,
Wade

The ship was sent to Newfoundland, steaming on one propeller, to have quick repairs. We returned to the operating area, and then:

Wednesday, July 15

Ray my dearest!
Darling, I still can't get over your news! I'm so proud of us I could bust!

You want to know how it feels to be an expecting father, honey? It feels good! In fact, I'll bet it feels exactly the same way as being an expectant mother!

I can hardly wait to see you feeding and washing our baby. Ray darling, you'll be the most beautiful most wonderful young mother there ever was.

If we have a boy, I guess we'll have to call him "George," and a girl "Georgia." Hey? After the Hotel St. George? I'm just kidding, honey, 'cause I feel so happy about our family. If I could only be with you now!

Raymonde, my angel wife, expecting fathers do worry, and I'm beginning to worry about you. Are you going to be alright? Will you go to a good doctor for a checkup every so often? Please! Sweetheart, take care of yourself!

You see, my Ray, I am completely and utterly in love with you—and I want you to live with me and love me and be my wife for all the rest of my days.

Love always, dearest,
Wade

This cruise ended in October, with the return of the ship to Brooklyn Navy Yard for maintenance.

While the ship was in Brooklyn, Raymonde and I lived in a garden apartment that she had rented. It was just two rooms and a kitchen, but it was our first chance to enjoy a real home life together. After a day at our respective jobs, our evening reunion was a delight. We spent the hours before lights-out reading, talking, smooching and planning for the future. At this time, Raymonde claimed that she didn't know how to cook (it caused shock in Richmond). In Brooklyn, however, she was a quick learner of basic meal preparation, aided by some French memories. A dish she called macaroni tambale was a particular favorite. These were precious days of domesticity and tranquility. About the only excitement came when she took driving lessons at a school in Manhattan–amidst all the traffic and wild taxi drivers–and earned her driving license.

Raymonde was four months pregnant at this time. I, aboard the ship, was scheduled to leave on cruise in January. We were considering that she might live in the New York area, using the St. Alban's Naval Hospital for obstetric care. She came back from one examination angry because the hospital corpsman said she was overweight–"I do not think they should let MEN in that service!"

Around this time, my mother threatened to come up to New York to stay with Raymonde. This was not a good idea, partly because Eliza Foy was not in good health. It was a difficult decision. Raymonde was a strong girl; she thought that in my absence she could handle herself with the help of friends. But she was also sure that she could not handle herself, the birth of our child, and her mother-in-law all together in New York. Thus, we decided that Raymonde would live in Richmond while the *Pursuit* was away.

The ship sailed in January 1953 for five months of hydrographic survey work in the Caribbean Sea. In February Raymonde left her job and moved to Richmond, residing in my family home. There she undertook to fit into the family style of living and to please my mother–a nearly impossible task. It was a difficult situation. From the Richmond family viewpoint, here was a "movie-star-gorgeous" young addition to the family whose experience in France and Switzerland was mostly beyond their understanding. Ever after, when Raymonde went to list her husband's sins, they started with, "And I had to spend a year in

Richmond with YOUR mother!"

There were compensations. Cousins Oma Welch and Mary Bruner had traveled quite a bit, and they took to Raymonde as great friends. My father loved her quietly from the beginning. Other members of the family, such as Mary Ellen Taylor, tried to make her welcome.

Still, the hot weather of Virginia was hard on a good Swiss girl, and the Southern style of cuisine was heavy (the Richmond folks could not understand why Raymonde did not gain weight). To make matters worse, the tension between her and Eliza Foy was continual. Raymonde was not about to be converted into a "Southern Belle" type. It made for a home-life with recurrent friction. On one occasion, at a physical checkup with the family physician, Raymonde broke down in tears. Dr. Blanton said, "She is not easy to live with, is she?"

Raymonde had love and regard for her own parents, but she had lost much of her respect for them. In the Foy family home there was an opportunity for my mother to give her extra affection and consideration. It did not happen. Indeed, it never even occurred to Eliza Foy to seek out friends fluent in French with whom Raymonde could enjoy conversation in her native language. The classic expression is, "Two women under the same roof equals great trouble." As it was, Raymonde mostly retired to writing letters to me and preparing for our baby's arrival.

All of this portrays my mother in a poor light. She meant well, but had her own ideas of the sort of apparel, speech and attitude that were appropriate for a young woman in the Old South. Eliza was not "simpatico," in the good Spanish meaning of the word, and Raymonde, after all she had been through, was no conformist. The opportunity for the two ladies to develop mutual understanding and a working relationship was not realized.

A beautiful little girl arrived on 3 March 1953: Virginia Elizabeth Foy. It was a very difficult labor. The obstetrician, Dr. M. Vitsky, left Raymonde in labor for far too long and finally delivered the baby by Caesarean section. The experience, without her husband there for support, left Raymonde exhausted and agonized. Only her love for little Ginny provided her a measure of comfort.

Out of the hospital and back at the Foy family home, Raymonde began maternal care. My mother was not much help, often finding fault with Raymonde's choice of the baby's apparel or choice of feeding time, etc. On the other hand, baby Ginny became the delight of Wade Senior's life. He would often come home early from the Pharmacy, put her in the stroller, and walk with her around the neighborhood, showing off. He even rolled on the floor, playing with her–something, it was noted, that he had not done with his own sons.

The ship returned to Norfolk in June. The Reed family, distant relatives and good friends, very graciously loaned us their home in Ocean View, so Raymonde and Ginny and I took up housekeeping there. We entertained friends from the ship, as well as Connie Reed and her mother. It was good to become accustomed to married life. We learned that sugar is a necessary ingredient in cherry pie, and that chopped garlic in cream cheese makes a tasty snack but keeps visitors a bit uncomfortable. It was a month of happiness, with only normal ship's work taking up some of my time.

This was also a time to plan for the future, as I would finish the normal two-year tour of active Naval Reserve duty in about five months. One of my options was to go back to work at General Electric Co. Another was to pursue further schooling. I considered the fact that for advanced engineering work I would need a higher university degree; Raymonde endorsed the goal. We both knew that it would mean a considerable period of time with low income but accepted the risk. Thus, I applied to Massachusetts Institute of Technology for admission as a graduate student in electrical engineering.

From July to October of 1953, the *Pursuit* was on hydrographic survey duty, again in Greenland waters, with me as executive officer and navigator. Raymonde and Ginny went back to reside in the Richmond family home. The ship was back in Brooklyn by the end of October, and Raymonde and I rented a friend's place on Staten Island for temporary residence. On 20 November I was admitted to MIT. Through the good offices of Professor Karl Wildes, I got an appointment as research assistant, as well as a place on the list of applicants for apartments in the married students' housing projects.

I was released from active duty in the Naval Reserve in December, and bid "goodbye" to the good ship USS *Pursuit*. After a stop in Richmond, Raymonde and I packed Ginny in our little blue Plymouth, loaded "all our worldly goods" in a rented trailer and headed for Massachusetts.

We arrived in Cambridge on 4 January 1954. It was a typical Boston area winter day–cold, cloudy, chilly

51

wind blowing and little piles of old snow with dirty black borders giving the landscape a dismal look. The married students' housing, named Westgate West, consisted of old, grey, two-story clapboard Army barracks, each of which had been converted into ten "apartments," a flattering term for these rundown units. The living quarters for a couple consisted of a living room, kitchen and dining nook, average-sized bedroom, small bedroom and bathroom. Heat came through a gas unit located in the living room; when another room was shut off from the living room it got no heat at all.

Raymonde and I inspected our first floor unit. One wall of the bedroom had been painted a streaked dark grey. Ginny crawled across the floor, and when we picked her up, her hands and knees were black with dirt. The previous tenants had left the place un-cleaned for a month. It was not a pleasing prospect. In fact, it was downright ugly.

This was not an auspicious introduction to our first reasonably stable home, but Raymonde took it in stride. I was not sure whether she accepted the mess because we would be together or because she was simply glad to get away from Richmond—perhaps it was some of both. But ever after I paid honor to my wife's courage and adaptability because of the strength with which she faced this daunting place.

It took a couple of days of washing, scrubbing and painting to make the place presentable. Our furniture was well used but serviceable. Raymonde was a good homemaker. She quickly met and mixed with the other ladies of our barracks; it was quite a cosmopolitan group with Swiss, Greek, Israeli and Armenian couples as well as American. Financial conditions were varied, the most affluent being the professional U.S. military people studying on assignment for advanced degrees. The ladies sometimes got together for evening kaffee-klatch. When Raymonde entertained, I either shut the door to the bedroom (where I studied) and froze, or left the door open to be distracted (and enlightened) by the conversation.

I took up my research assistantship in the MIT Servomechanisms Laboratory, under a good section head, John Brean. The Laboratory projects were electronic applications sponsored by the U.S. Department of Defense. In my section were two full-time staff engineers and three others on assistantships.

Time off regular hours was given for attendance at classes. I had two courses each quarter. My instructors were excellent; of particular note was Prof. H. E. Edgerton for Electronic Instrumentation. Asst. Prof. F. B. Hildebrand, Advanced Calculus, became my model for a mathematics instructor: logical and well-organized lectures, lots of homework problems, comprehensive and challenging examinations.

Engineering research was active during these years. Control system theory in particular was making major advances. Transistors, based on electronic conduction in solid-state structures, were coming into use and replacing vacuum tubes in radios, computers and everything in between.

Appraisal of our eighteen-month stay at MIT is not easy. The external appearance of the grey barracks buildings was grubby at best, and Boston weather was often depressingly cheerless. It was not easy to keep the little apartment clean and neat. Certainly one looked around and did not get the feeling that "every prospect pleases." With a tight budget there was not a lot we could do to relieve the dull aspect.

Occasionally we, with Ginny, could make a day trip to visit friends like the Taylors at Hopewell Junction. We had weekend visitors at various times: Uncle Adrian, my brother Tom and his family. On a happy spring-break visit to Richmond, Raymonde completed her probation period for immigration. Her papers, having shifted around New York and Pasadena and other mysterious places (and having been delayed because of her marriage), finally found their way to Richmond after Wade Senior called in some favors from the Postmaster General. Raymonde had her immigration interview with a judge, passing at least partly because of her total honesty. Some family member with good intentions had asked an acquaintance who was thought to have influence to go to the interview and grease the legal ways, but when asked by the judge, Raymonde said, "I've never seen this man before." On 19 April 1954, she took the oath and became a citizen of the U.S.A. As she said, "It's about time. I am married to a U.S. Naval officer and am the mother of a U.S. citizen!" It was a day of pride and celebration.

In our barracks at MIT were several good neighbors. The couples were nearly all in the same boat—studies, work, children, low-to-middle income levels. There was a married students' organization in Westgate West that ran a babysitting pool—Raymonde or I would do babysitting duty for another couple, earning credit hours, and when we needed to go out, the pool would call someone to sit with Ginny. This allowed Raymonde to take part-time X-ray work; her department head was Dr. Alice Ettinger, an eminent MD and a truly gracious lady who became a good friend. Raymonde and I also took advantage of the pool to attend to "cultural improvement;" indeed, looking back, we realized that we went to the symphony, opera and ballet more often during our year and a half at MIT than in any other comparable period of our lives. Boston had something to offer besides grey skies and dirty snow.

Despite its lack of elegance, the little apartment became a home. Raymonde and I could expect to be together for as much of the future as we could foresee. Our situation was stable, and toddler Ginny was a delight. Together we learned a lot about keeping house. Cooking was something of an adventure. Once we tried batter bread with a Southern recipe–it looked too gooey, so we added flour, and it came out of the oven hard as a brick. Another time we brought home a pair of lobsters. The beasts got loose on the kitchen floor and strolled around clicking their claws threateningly. It took considerable effort to round them up and get them into the pot.

At one point Raymonde and Ginny made a short trip to Los Angeles to visit the van Laars in Pasadena. Charles and Dichette were happy to see their granddaughter.

Our experience at MIT marked the true beginning of our family life. Raymonde and I showered Ginny with attention and affection. Raymonde was especially lovely. The mutual attraction between us grew. Our love strengthened and blossomed.

MIT was also a success in professional terms. In May Raymonde took and passed the American

Society of X-ray Technicians tests for licensing. She was then a Registered X-ray Technologist. My work in the Servomechanisms Laboratory went well, my studies also. On 21 September 1955, I was awarded the degree Master of Science in Electrical Engineering. Raymonde and I considered our options. I was interested in research, so we decided I should go for a doctor's degree. We might have stayed at MIT, but a somewhat rash impulse led us to seek a school located near Pasadena and Raymonde's parents. I applied for and was admitted to graduate studies at the California Institute of Technology.

5

🌸

1955 – 1962
ALTADENA AND BALTIMORE

Moving a household is never easy, even for a relatively bare and mobile outfit, and Raymonde and I never were very good at it. In late summer, 1955, we trekked with Ginny across the country, all in our little blue Plymouth sedan, towing a rental trailer with furniture and other household items. The travel was brightened by a two-day visit with Lydia and Carl Glock in Pittsburgh; Dorothy and Ralph Griswold also came to call.

The drive across the country was something of an ordeal–fatiguing, mostly boring–in which the major object of each day was to cover as much territory as we could without irritating each other to the point of nasty behavior. There were points of interest–crossing the "Father of Waters," sighting clearly the High Sierra– but sightseeing was a low priority, and so our strongest memory was of how deadly long it took to drive across Kansas. Raymonde and I shared the driving duties; it was a tribute to our mutual respect that neither of us tried to "side-seat drive" the other (at least, not too often). Ginny dozed or squirmed in the rear seat. At the end of the day a motel room provided temporary shelter for a relaxation of tensions and some relief from the car. The trip was not particularly enjoyable or enlightening.

Arriving in Pasadena, Raymonde, Ginny and I first stayed in the van Laars' home with Charles, Dichette and Dolly. Raymonde made a big effort to please her parents. I wasn't much help; Dichette and I established a sort of "armed-truce" relationship. Charles was busy teaching languages, first at a private school and later at Pasadena City College. Dolly was doing nursing work at a local hospital. Dolly's animosity for her sister was always present. All of us had affection for Ginny, which helped soothe any immediate ruptures.

After a short search, Raymonde and I bought a small one-story house at 494 Colman Street in Altadena, a suburb north of Pasadena. It had two bedrooms, a living room, a dining room, kitchen and one bath. The siding was redwood, the roof was wood shakes; it had a covered patio, a carport and a narrow, fairly large fenced yard with some fruit trees.

This place, of course, was our first venture in real estate and the initial "nest-of-our-own." It was anything but handsome in appearance. In fact, while considered a ranch-style house, it might also have been called an upscale range shack. But the van Laars did approve. The important thing was that we all three now had room to stretch ourselves, to develop day-to-day working routines and to grow closer to one another. It took a while for us to organize the house cleaning, yard maintenance, child care, automobile care, studying, child education, food provision, recreational activities and necessary loving time into a satisfactory division of labor. We had some disagreements, but our three-way state of mutual affection created an environment in which disciplined cooperation was the customary mode of operation.

We moved in our furnishings and borrowed a couple of extra pieces from the van Laars. We cleaned the place, hung curtains, arranged the kitchen and dining equipment and made the little house livable. There was a sense of partnership and accomplishment when Raymonde and I worked together, even if it only amounted to stirring up a lot of dust. We undertook to improve the landscaping and gardening, and found in the process that planting in Southern California was not easy. It involved wetting a spot of dirt, scooping out the mud, pouring more water in the hole, grubbing out more mud and repeating these steps until the proper depth was reached. Then you could set the plant in the ground with a bucketful of potting soil. I would get this done, and then Raymonde, like any good woman, would come over and say, "It doesn't fit there–wrong color/shape/pattern/size. Move it six feet." This would produce a lot of questionable language that only stopped when she kissed me.

The next-door neighbors, Mr. and Mrs. J. Murray, became good friends. After a while we found a pre-kindergarten school for Ginny, and Raymonde took on part-time work in X-ray at Huntington Hospital. She met Mary Sperling, who became a friend. Raymonde was happy enough with our little home that we entertained fairly often. We had the Murrays over for dinners, and the Sperlings came for some weekend afternoons. Mary's husband, Herbert, was a notable artist-photographer with movie industry contacts and a sizeable fund of stories. By sticking to California wines, I acquired a highly undeserved reputation as a connoisseur. With considerable courage we had Charles and Dichette, and sometimes Dolly, visit for a lunch or dinner; the results were usually pleasant, and it can be recorded that there were no occasions that required the fire department to be called. Through the van Laars, we acquired more friends: Miriam Delp, the Walter Riddells.

"Greater Los Angeles" was a sprawling monstrosity of a community, featuring such "low-culture" attractions as Hollywood and Disneyland. Pasadena was in some sense an appendage, but also an independent city. A major event was the annual Tournament of Roses Parade held on New Year's Day. In its early years, the parade had been composed of Southern California marching bands, horseback riding clubs and civic organizations that entered floats covered in flowers; by the 1950s, though, it had grown into a national occasion, with agencies competing for prizes for the best floats. We went both years that we were in Altadena, showing up early to get good seats in the stands or on the curb. Ginny took delight in the bright colors, the music and the people who would wave to her from the floats.

Much of the Pasadena population was elderly, and the good ladies were active in literary groups. One day at a crosswalk downtown, Raymonde observed from her car several old folks slowly making their way across the street. She remarked, "Look at the Shakespeare Club on the loose!" Her mother thought it was not respectful.

I went to work at CalTech on a teaching assistantship under Prof. McCann, the Electrical Engineering Department head, and took a full course load. I had some good instructors but managed just a B-C level in my studies. Holding laboratory exercises for undergraduate students was somewhat difficult and time consuming, partly due to the lack of instruction manuals for the equipment. In mid-academic-year came calamity; on the final examination of a required course on Static and Dynamic Electricity, taught by Physics Prof. W. R. Smythe, I panicked, flunking the exam and the course (this was actually strange–the first and last time such a panic struck). As a result, by spring of 1956, it was obvious that I would not complete work on a doctor's degree at CalTech any time soon. Our funds were running short, so Raymonde and I realized that plans for my schooling would have to be put on hold. I would have to go out and do some honest, real-world work.

There were local opportunities for an engineer at North American Aviation, for instance, but the work did not appear to be of the type that I wanted. Among my responses to several advertisements, one drew an offer from Glenn L. Martin Co. in Baltimore, Maryland. The work seemed to be challenging: aircraft design, analysis and computer applications. The salary was reasonable, and the offer included payment for moving. Raymonde had more than a few reservations about a move back to the East Coast, but I had my way and accepted the Martin offer.

October 1956 was a busy month. A moving van carried our belongings away from Altadena; the little blue Plymouth sedan was left with Dolly. Raymonde, Ginny and I flew to Baltimore, stopped for a couple of weeks in a rented apartment, bought a car and looked for a place to stay. One day, sightseeing in the city, we took a bus ride to see the Martin Co. office-plant complex at Middle River. It was a mistake, as the bus route went through some of the worst sections of town. I half expected Raymonde to demand to go straight back to Southern California, but she didn't.

It looked as if we would be in the East for a while, so we decided to plunge into real estate again (we had not lost too much on the Altadena property). With the help of Miss Lucie Mansfield, realtor, we found a place we could afford at 7016 Kenleigh Road in Stoneleigh, a north-Baltimore suburban community. It was a two-and-a-half-story "colonial" model with white stucco siding, slate roof and a basement, as well as three bedrooms, one bath, living room, dining room and kitchen. The "half-story" was a den tacked onto the rear. For comparison, the price came to $17 per square foot of living area, whereas in Altadena it was $14 per square foot. The lot was large and green, with mature trees and a fenced back yard. A one-car garage was set close to the house. Gardening in Maryland was far easier than in California, despite the summer heat and humidity.

At Martin Co. my department head was Floyd Nixon, a good man, a top-notch engineer and the author of a textbook on control system design. The department's job was to use both analog and digital computers to study the dynamics and flight characteristics of the airplanes and missiles built by the company. My first assignment was on the Vanguard project under Ernie Loft. This was an early satellite-launch vehicle. I did an analysis of the orbit-injection stage that was a significant contribution. The first two launch attempts failed, with spectacular news coverage. The third launch vehicle sent into orbit the second U.S. satellite. Now a Vanguard rocket is on display in the Smithsonian Air and Space Museum. Later work of mine, under Dr. Wilhelm Elfers and with engineer Gene Lefferts, turned out well. I contributed to proposals and did analyses for a variety of projects over the years.

Two years into my time at Martin, the company instituted a program, in conjunction with Drexel Institute of Philadelphia, to implement night classes for graduate degrees. I became an instructor and taught a course: Functions of a Complex Variable.

With company endorsement, I applied in February 1957 for admission to The Johns Hopkins University in Baltimore as a part-time graduate student in electrical engineering. I was accepted in March and started in September, taking time from regular working hours to attend day classes. Thus, both gainful employment and academic progress were well underway.

Raymonde was occupied with making a home for the three of us. She was good at it. In Baltimore shops and used furniture stores she found several pieces of good, sturdy, classic furniture that made for graceful living. We had good neighbors. Miss Artus James, a neighbor lady of the Old School, took a special interest in Raymonde. Mary Will was an affable next-door neighbor, and Dr. and Mrs. Herman Praguer were friends with European backgrounds. I joined a car pool for work, so Raymonde was mobile for all but one day a week. She, Ginny and I settled down and had a normal family life with only the average number of bumps along the way. Friends—Mid and Clay Taylor, Doug Rumble and his wife Althea—came for short visits. Living was good.

Our home was just a quick drive from Annapolis. At that time a major event of the U.S. Naval Academy June Week was the Farewell Ball, to which all Navy couples were welcome. For several years Raymonde and I drove to Annapolis for the gala outing. The event was held on the USNA campus in MacDonogh Hall, a building with a high ceiling and large floor that was sometimes used for indoor infantry drill. On the night of the ball, it would be decorated with signal flags and patriotic colors. Some members of the Academy faculty and staff formed a receiving line down which Raymonde and I progressed–she, lovely in formal dress, and I, choking in my high-collared white Reserve uniform. We roamed through the crowd of uniformed midshipmen, ladies in beautiful ball gowns and other guests. The band played swing, waltzes and fox trots. We enjoyed the dancing and impressive ambiance. After the last note of Sleepy Time Gal and the departing rush of the girls and their midshipmen escorts, we strolled out into the town and drove home.

Another event we attended one year was the Army-Navy football game in Philadelphia–cold, crowded, noisy, colorful. Raymonde was not well versed in U.S. style football–"a RUDE game." She found herself cheering by mistake for Army as much as for Navy. She was, however, greatly impressed by the marching of the Corps of Cadets and the Brigade of Midshipmen; the pageantry of the event was remarkable. And we both just managed to avoid frostbite.

Baltimore is close enough to Richmond that we could still visit with my family. Some of these visits were pleasant and some produced friction, but not often enough to create too much distress. Then in 1957, after a fight with prostate cancer, my father died. My mother stayed on in the family home, with only Mary Cheatham, the cook, for company. After some years this arrangement was no longer tenable and Eliza moved to an apartment in a long-term care complex. The Foy family home on Chamberlayne Avenue was demolished and replaced with an apartment building.

With a stable home, work going well and Ginny running around happily, Raymonde and I faced a major decision. We both wanted another child, but we knew that Raymonde would not be able to have a normal delivery. She remembered vividly the pain and stress of Ginny's birth. It was Raymonde's decision, but I did apply a little gentle influence. Knowing the danger to her life, and much aware of the labor agony and post-operative pain she could expect, still she decided to have a second baby.

I was aware that Raymonde would have difficulty but had no personal experience to guide me. As I came to realize her fear and apprehension, I began to comprehend just how brave and strong she was to make such a decision. My love and admiration for my wife grew beyond all bounds. She was a true heroine.

Pregnancy followed soon enough, along with the usual morning sickness and discomfort. In the winter of 1958, her time arrived. I took Raymonde to the hospital, saw her put to bed and kissed her good night. She was frightened but kept her nerve. In the early morning hours she began bleeding and called the nurse. Her obstetrician, Dr. A. Milan, was at the hospital and came directly to her aid. On 20 February 1958, he delivered, by Caesarean section, a fine little baby boy. In this way, Wade Charles van Laar Foy arrived in the world. When I saw them in the morning, both mother and son were doing well. Raymonde could even smile at her husband. Dr. Milan's attentive and professional care was exemplary, and we acknowledged this with gratitude.

When Raymonde and I brought little Charles home, Ginny looked at him and wondered what justified all the fuss. The four of us, however, had a happy home; strains were eased with proper discipline and plenty of love. As Ginny and Charles grew, they actually got along quite well together. When it came time, she went to the grade school about half-a-block from our home. During the summers, Stoneleigh opened a community swimming pool that we all enjoyed.

Baltimore weather is variable: March snowstorms, summer heat waves. I came home one day during a particularly loud thunderstorm to find Raymonde and Ginny hiding under a bed; they did not appreciate my laughter. During this time, for some reason that I did not understand, we acquired a striped grey cat, Kitchy-Koo. I thought this was carrying domesticity a bit far, but Ginny and Chuck were delighted.

At Johns Hopkins my studies went well. I had excellent instructors: Prof. Willis Gore for Electronic Design, Jan Minkowski for Physics of Semiconductors, Prof. Haviland for Probability Theory. Professor William Huggins taught Signal Design. He and Prof. Gore became my thesis advisors. A particularly enjoyable course, which I took for "cultural-horizon-expanding" reasons, was Medieval Economic History under Prof. Frederic Lane.

Business was good at Martin, which merged with Marietta Co. around 1958. We won the contract to develop the Pershing missile for the U.S. Army, and the company set up a facility for that purpose in Orlando, Florida. Floyd Nixon and Dr. Will Elfers moved there to take on important jobs. I was asked to go with them, but considered my studies at Johns Hopkins to be too far advanced to be broken off; besides, Raymonde was well situated in Baltimore and had no high opinion of Florida. The department at Martin, Baltimore was taken over by Dr. Peter Myers, another very good man.

The decade starting in 1960 was one of notable social change in the U.S. It marked the end of the Dwight Eisenhower presidency, which led to the constitutional amendment restricting any person to two presidential terms. John F. Kennedy was elected president, the Civil Rights Act of 1960 was enacted, and the U.S. involvement in the Vietnam War escalated. In Baltimore, Raymonde and I were occupied with work, raising Ginny and Chuck, and home management. We followed the news, voted regularly and were conscientious members of the Republican Party, but had little engagement in political activity. I was handling a full-time job at Martin and was teaching evening class twice a week in the Drexel-Martin program. It left little time to scratch.

In 1960 I applied for and was awarded a National Science Foundation fellowship. With its support, I took leave without pay from Martin Co. and spent the academic year from September 1960 to June 1961 in full-time studies at Johns Hopkins. I could take the streetcars along Charles Street, a few blocks from home, for transportation to and from the University. On some cold days, Raymonde sent me off with a small flask of rum for warmth and "stimulation of the brain cells." Early in this period, I took my oral examination before a panel of professors for admission to doctoral candidacy—an affair of an hour or so that I passed, but that left me wringing wet with perspiration. I then proceeded with research on an aspect of information theory and wrote my thesis.

All this time Raymonde was a strong supporter, taking care of Ginny and Chuck, keeping the home in good shape and arranging for me to have time to study. Thus, when I was granted my Doctor of Engineering degree in January 1962, Raymonde had definitely earned her PHT for "Pushing Hubby Through!"

Having achieved our academic goal and having established a fair record in engineering work, Raymonde and I took stock of our affairs. The children were growing up. Ginny was doing well in third grade with no close local ties. Chuck was an adventuresome little fellow who liked to ride off on his tricycle exploring the neighborhood. My work at Martin was interesting and productive but was becoming somewhat routine. It seemed likely that before long Raymonde's parents would be in need of some assistance. In short, a case of itchy feet developed, and we decided to look for new work on the West Coast.

My responses to advertised openings drew two offers of interviews. Raymonde and I flew to San Francisco to visit Stanford Research Institute. Then I went to Seattle (a spectacular flight) to visit Boeing Aircraft, while Raymonde flew to Los Angeles to visit her parents. The work to be done at Boeing was similar to what I was doing at Martin. The institute, SRI, was a non-profit contract research house of some 1000 scientists, engineers and business people with a variety of projects. It was located in Menlo Park, one patch in the crazy quilt of communities that extends from San Francisco south along the west Bay Shore. The research work in physics and engineering was of high quality. A typical project would last for about a year, so one would have little opportunity to get bored with the "same old thing all the time." I was offered a job as Research Engineer in the Radio Systems Laboratory under Dean Babcock, a good man with contacts in several U.S. government agencies. Raymonde and I decided to take the SRI job, made peace with the people at Martin Co. and made preparations to leave for California.

A review of our six years in Baltimore is in order. At the beginning our finances were low. We had lived within our income from assistantships and the GI Bill, and so had avoided debt. Raymonde referred to that period as "when we were poor like rats!" I had a small inheritance from Aunt Belle Taylor, and we had saved a good bit from the Navy pay; this provided the down payments on our houses. We lost some money on the sale of the ranch house in Altadena and would also lose on the home in Stoneleigh. We had saved carefully while I was employed at Martin. In 1962, then, Raymonde and I stood on rather solid financial ground with a reasonable amount of savings and a good prospect for future income.

Neither of us had formed much attachment to the city of Baltimore. Its waterfront (since renovated) had little to offer in the way of attractions, and the blocks of nearly identical brick row houses did not possess much architectural charm. We had good neighbors in Stoneleigh, a community that was distinctive in several ways. For example, the principal of the local high school, against vehement opposition, vetoed the fielding of a school football team. He took the position that "Any activity that requires its players to be armored is not appropriate for teenage boys." Raymonde and I always admired the intelligence and courage it took for him to make such a decision.

In professional terms there had been well-founded advancement. In 1962, I was an experienced engineer, particularly in scientific computer work. To have attained the Doctor's degree was a major accomplishment in both academic and practical careers. We had both respect and good feeling for the Martin Co., where we had found so many good people to work with and for. The Johns Hopkins University would always hold a warm place in our hearts. Raymonde and I could look back on six years of progress.

Moreover, we had rounded out our family. Ginny was a good, happy girl, doing her schoolwork and trying all sorts of things from sledding to informal ballet. Chuck was a cute, growing boy. We always remembered him coming inside from playing in the snow—ice all around his hood, tears frozen on his cheeks, fingers out of his mittens and stiff with cold. It would take half an hour to get him out of his snowsuit and to get him warm—then he would be ready to go out again.

Raymonde and I tangled at times. After acquiring a television, I took a dim view of spending much time watching it—"That thing will turn your spine to spaghetti and your brain to mush!" Once the set broke down and, when I dawdled getting it fixed, Raymonde and the kids were angry with me.

Such spats did not last, though. Raymonde and I were deeply in love. A warm glance and smile, the surge of desire, an hour of quiet and privacy, and our lovemaking would leave us warm, happy and conjoined.

The Baltimore period, then, was a time of career growth and personal and familial enrichment. If such an analogy is not too far-fetched, you could say that our prosperity trace had undergone a positive acceleration bump.

A van Laar family portrait: Dolly, Charles, Tommy, Dichette and Raymonde.
Taken around 1930 in Gerzensee, Switzerland.

Raymonde, age 7, 1929.

Raymonde and Dichette in Switzerland in the 1930s.

Raymonde on the horse Whiskey in Villers-sur-Mer, France around 1937.

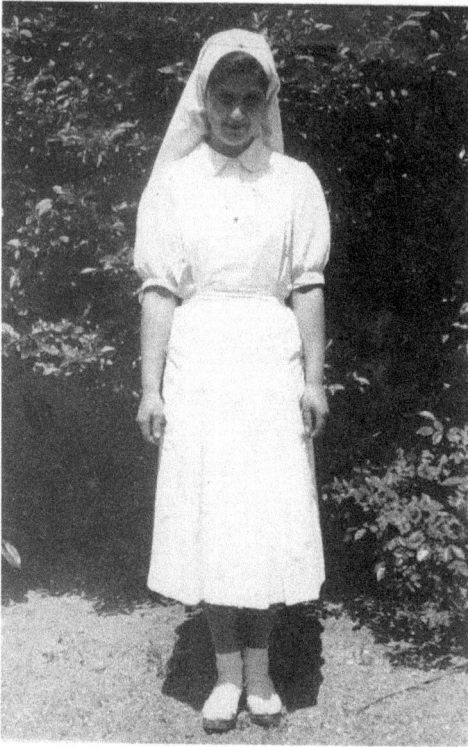

Raymonde wearing her nurse's uniform in Bayonne, France in the 1940s.

Raymonde's nursing certificate from the French Red Cross.

Raymonde playing the accordion for passengers on the M.S. *Veendam* during the family's ten-day voyage to the U.S. in June of 1947.

May 19, 1952: Raymonde and Wade's wedding. Matron of honor Mildred Taylor, Raymonde, Reverend Maclaren Boyden, Wade and best man Tom Foy.

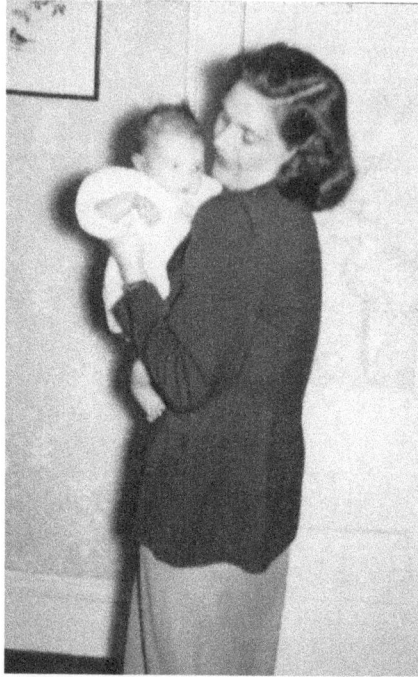

Raymonde with new baby Virginia in 1953.

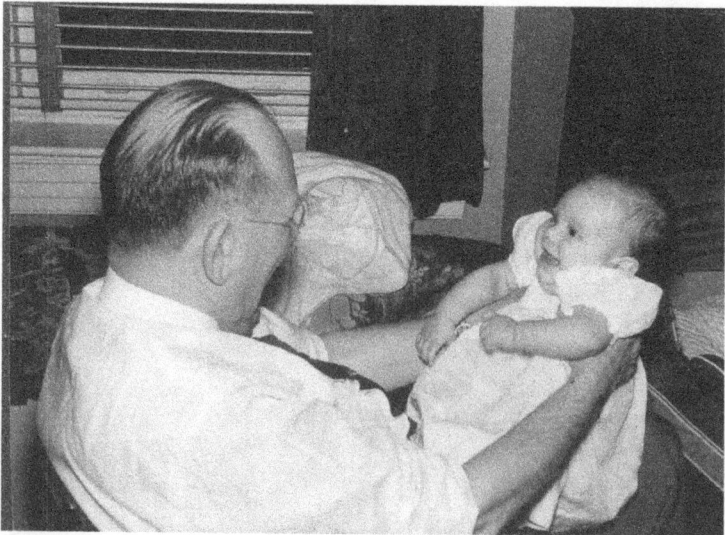

Wade Sr. and Ginny, aged 8 months, at the Foy family home on
Chamberlayne Ave. in Richmond, 1953.

Raymonde and Ginny at Ocean View, Virginia in 1953.

A glamour shot: Raymonde during their stay at Ocean View in 1953.

Easter Day, 1954. Raymonde and Ginny at the married students' housing project at MIT.

Raymonde dressed up. Taken around 1954, when the family was living at MIT.

April 19th, 1954: A brand new U.S. citizen.
Raymonde emerges from court after taking her
oath of citizenship.

Easter Day, 1960. Ginny, Ramonde and Chuck outside their home in Baltimore.

Thanksgiving Day, 1962: Charles, Dichette, Raymonde, Ginny and Chuck in Pasadena, California.

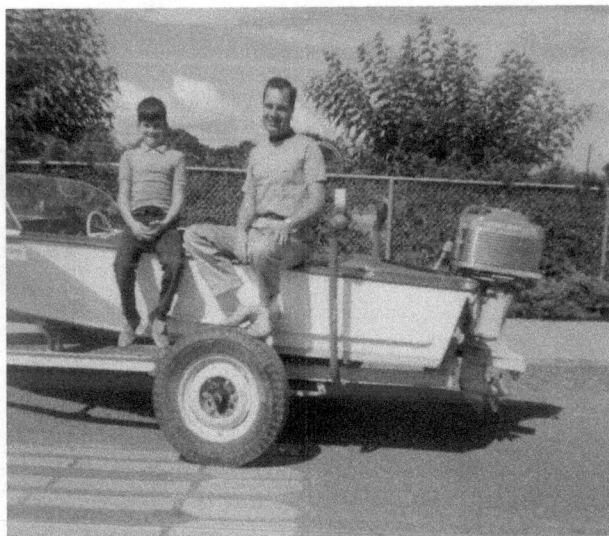

Wade and Chuck on the family's boat, which they bought used, repaired and took waterskiing. Taken in April of 1969 in Los Altos, California.

A portrait of Raymonde from 1975.

Raymonde and Wade "getting settled" at home in Los Altos in the 1960s.

October 1, 1983: Virginia and Mathew's wedding. Wade, Raymonde, Vivian Streeter (Mathew's mother), Mathew, Ginny, Maureen Ross (Mathew's sister) and Mike Reed (best man).

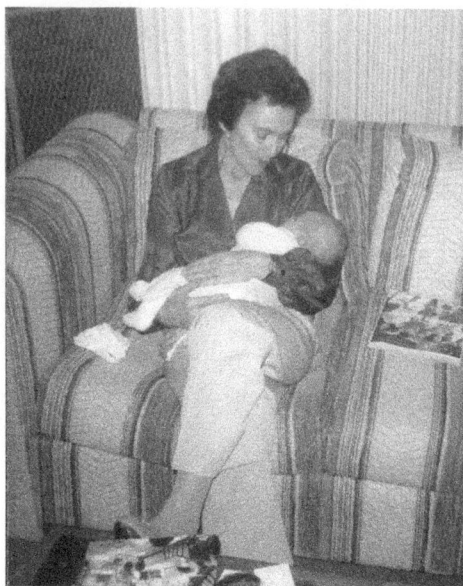

Raymonde and new grandson Zachary, aged 12
days, in San Diego in 1984.

"Marvelous people:" Lydia and Carl Glock at their home in Pittsburgh in 1966.

Raymonde's old school friend Kitty Belle with husband Tom Steiger at home in Mercersburg, PA in the 1990 s. Taken by Raymonde and Wade during a visit to the Steigers' cattle farm.

Raymonde and Aunt Madeleine on a tour boat on Lake Geneva ("Lac Léman") in 1970.

Raymonde's uncle Andre Petitmaitre in Switzerland in the 1980s.

Raymonde and her cousin Eric Auckenthaler in Annecy, France in 2000.

A photograph of the van Laar estate in Gerzensee, taken
on a trip in the 1990s.

Raymonde with grandson Zachary in 1999.

6

🌸

1962 – 1990
LOS ALTOS

Again came a drive across the U.S. in the summer of 1962. For this trip, the household furniture went by moving van, which made travel easier. But also now Ginny and Chuck were old enough to get into trouble, so every so often the rear seat would erupt in a squabble. It was good that in those days there were no back-seat seatbelt laws; otherwise, the restraints on young folks' squirming might have been intolerable. The cat stayed under a seat, in hiding.

My most vivid memory of the drive was of a Wyoming motel. I woke up in the middle of the night and my wife was gone! Looking around outside I found Raymonde, half asleep, walking the grey cat, Kitchy Koo, on a leash. I think we were both in a state of mild shock as a result of driving boredom.

In California we arrived with a heat wave. I rented a Palo Alto house for a year. It was a type of "Eichler house" that had spread through the area over the past few years—one-story, flat roof, built on a concrete slab with "radiant" heating. Raymonde took one look at it and, like a good Swiss girl, thought, "What happens if an ice accumulation gets too heavy? What happens

88

if the rain can't find a way to run off? What happens if an earthquake cracks the slab?" She said to herself, "We are not going to stay in this thing any longer than necessary!" So, Raymonde went house hunting.

In Los Altos, one of the suburban communities in the Peninsula south of San Francisco, she found a one-story, ranch-type dwelling: long, stucco siding, lots of room, redwood paneling in the interior, roof of asphalt shingles, extra large lot, attached garage, fir trees in the front, picture windows in the dining and living rooms, magnolia tree in back, small separate workshop with a carport. I grumbled, of course, noting, "The price per square foot of living area is greater than we paid in Baltimore." Raymonde insisted that she liked it best of all the places she had seen. She had her way, and the purchase of 214 E. Edith Avenue was far and away the best investment we ever made. We moved in, had plenty of space for our good old furniture from Baltimore, and Raymonde proceeded to make it attractive and cheerful—nice curtains, separate rooms for Ginny and Chuck, space for the cat to roam, a handsome dining room, a workshop converted to a guest room and bath, wisteria over the back porch. She looked around and felt pride—it was *her* place. We had achieved financial stability; I was out of my student days and had good career prospects. Raymonde was in a home of her own—not someone else's room or apartment—and could expect to stay there as long as she wanted. I suspect a strong sense of peace, quiet happiness and delight crept into her soul at this time.

Stanford Research Institute, being a non-profit organization, had semi-academic status. One consequent advantage was that retirement funds were in the Teachers' Insurance and Annuity Association and the College Retirement Equities Fund; a wise-guy once remarked that the biggest benefit was that no SRI executive had any control over these funds. It took a while for me to realize that a non-profit organization had a very narrow financial road; the law did not allow profit, and the Board of Directors did not allow loss. At the top, SRI's directors were the Board of Trustees of Stanford University.

During my time at SRI, the U.S. went to war in Vietnam and anti-war protesting broke out on the campus. Some of the University students and faculty took violent objection to the SRI research work that was sponsored by the U.S. Department of Defense. It went far enough that a miscellaneous crowd "marched" on the institute campus. Together with SRI colleagues, I went into the bunch of protestors and defended the SRI policies. The confrontation was boisterous, but no one resorted to fisticuffs. The agitation precipitated a split between the university and the research institute. In the "divorce" settlement the institute agreed to pay a large alimony, drop the name "Stanford" and set up its own board of directors. It changed its name to SRI International. Somebody noted that putting the SRI legal staff against that of the university was like sending mice to run down Tom Cat Alley.

Raymonde and I settled in at our Los Altos home, adapting easily to the good weather and accommodating somewhat less easily to California manners. We had good neighbors like Mary Hedges across the street; Connie and Joe Bosza and Mary and Ed Simkins were also nearby. A French couple named Annik and Jean-Pierre Doutriaux took up housing in the neighborhood, having moved to the area to work for a couple of years. They gave Raymonde a chance to practice her French. The children's schools and the Main Street "downtown" district were fairly close. Raymonde took over the housekeeping and gardening, doing her usual good job. She also took charge of the cats. One day I saw Ginny and Chuck coming along the street with a furry, black bundle. They said, "Look at Othello, Daddy!" It turned out to be a she and was christened Jezebel–an apt name for this mischievous spitfire of a feline. She became a family treasure for years.

At SRI, I worked for good men, first Dean Babcock and later Dr. Larry Sweeney. My coworkers were Ed Elpel, the best engineer I ever knew, and Dr. Charles Dawson, among others. There were projects for the Army, the Navy and the Air Force. I was proficient at mathematics and control system analysis. I led some challenging and technically advanced projects, including one that required the development and test of a special analysis system; it involved selection and purchase of a dedicated computer, processing incoming data in real time, and writing the needed software in computer assembly language.

A series of projects we conducted for the Federal Aviation Administration under Joseph Cox took on the problem of large aircraft landing in the presence of "wind shear." This happened when an aircraft, heading into the wind for landing, suddenly had the wind shift to a cross–or tail–wind, causing a loss of lift. It had caused several bad accidents, commercial and military. Dean Babcock, myself and our team programmed some typical wind conditions and conducted trials on flight simulators at Douglas Aircraft and NASA Ames Research Center, using a detailed model of a Boeing 727, with volunteer pilots from the Air Force, the Navy and several major airlines. It was found that a prediction of the likelihood of wind shear could be made–the presence of a nearby thunderstorm, for example, was one contributing factor. We determined that the pilots should not throttle back when making a landing approach under possible wind-shear conditions; they might need the quick application of full thrust if danger threatened. This practice makes for hard impacts on the runway surface but provides a significant margin of safety.

A fair amount of travel was necessary, mostly to the East Coast and sometimes to Europe. While I was away on one trip, Raymonde came home to find that the house had been robbed, thieves having taken the silver tea-and-coffee set among other items. When I returned she said, "Why does the trouble always happen when *you* are away?" The Los Altos police were notified and an officer investigated. He told us that they knew the thief lived in the neighborhood but they could not prove anything; it did not recover our loss.

Among the work at other SRI engineering departments was a notable succession of contracts for the U.S. Defense Advanced Research Projects Agency. They included contracts at several universities and other research institutes. The originators and motivators at DARPA were Drs. J. C. R. Licklider and Lawrence Roberts. The SRI department head was Dr. Charles Rosen. In the course of the work, the teams developed data-packet switching, computer-to-computer communications, an ARPANET of interconnected computers and file-transfer protocols. These projects led, with contributions by V. Cerf, T. Berners-Lee and others, to the development of the Internet we use today.

On the advice of Dr. Dawson, and with the permission of SRI, I undertook part-time teaching at Santa Clara University. The School of Engineering offered graduate (MS and PhD level) courses in an early bird program. A class typically met twice a week from 7:10 to 9:00 a.m., so a student with a BS degree could, by taking two courses a quarter, advance to an MS in about three years without losing much time from his regular job. I taught in the Applied Mathematics Department under Prof. Gerald Markle, one of the finest men I ever knew. The subjects I taught most often were Partial Differential Equations and Applications of Linear Operators. It was good teaching—highly motivated students, small class sizes, fascinating subjects—and I was good at it. I was particularly fortunate to teach some students, like Nebosha Gacic of Yugoslavia, who displayed brilliance. Throughout this teaching endeavor, Raymonde was a source of continual encouragement. I would drag myself into the kitchen at about 6:00 on a class morning and find a note like:

"Mon cheri, coffee is made. Have a good lecture. I adore you. Ray
Please have a croissant."

This was a good way to get a fellow going early.

This was a time when "Silicon Valley" was developing. Companies such as Fairchild Semiconductor, Hewlett-Packard, Intel and Apple Computer were enjoying success. Graduate engineers and physicists were in demand. I remember hearing some of my students bragging about moving to a new job every six months.

Now Ginny and Chuck were growing up. They went through the Los Altos public schools, all fairly close to home, with average records and reasonable progress. When they stumbled in a class, Raymonde went directly to the teacher for explanations and corrective measures. They took a range of courses in high school, including classics and college preparation. In June 1971, Ginny graduated, having been the Student Body Secretary and taking a roll in the senior play. Charles graduated early in 1976, having earned his athletic letter in varsity soccer (an achievement his father had never accomplished).

It was about this time that Chuck discovered an interest in remote-control model airplanes. He became accomplished at construction and at flying them. These activities did a lot to use up his energy and enhance his practical education. They also meant that often the family room, kitchen and most of the rest of the house were reeking with the smell of airplane glue and torn foam plastic. On some weekend days the backyard was loud with the noise of one-cylinder engines and the bad language that accompanied attempts to get the things to start. Remarkably, the neighbors did not complain.

After high school the kids went to Foothill, the local community college–Ginny from 1971 to 1973, graduating with an Associate of Arts degree, and Chuck in the spring and summer of 1976. It was here, faced with Foothill's emphasis on academic excellence, that their entire approach to studies was reoriented and they determined to make the most of their college work.

To a considerable extent both these young people were victims of a faulty educational philosophy, even though the Los Altos public schools were some of the best in the area. There were foolish precepts:

Learning must be fun.

Mathematics can be taught by playing games.

Memorization is intellectually bad.

A student has a right to learn at his own pace.

Such ideas produced classes in which the teachers taught those who wanted to learn and let all the others coast. It was not until Ginny and Charles each reached Foothill College, where an English teacher, for example, flunked any essay with more than two spelling errors, that they began to take studies seriously and to use their good minds. Another source of distraction was the tendency then to introduce political influence into the classroom subject matter, particularly in high school. This aroused Raymonde's ire and she mounted an active campaign to counter it.

Each year the family made a couple of trips to Pasadena to visit Raymonde's parents. The drives were not hard and the young ones did enjoy the attention of their grandparents. On one such visit we got to watch a New Year's Day parade of the Tournament of Roses. Then, in November 1966, Dichette van Laar went to the hospital and succumbed to complications from diabetes. Her son and daughters gathered in Pasadena. Raymonde took on the tasks of dealing with the doctors, the hospital and the funeral arrangements; she did her usual conscientious job. Neither Dolly nor Charles was particularly grateful.

These years also permitted time for family vacation activities. The young ones and I tried camping, starting at Sunset Beach not far from home. We returned tired, with some discomfort and some happy experiences, and without major cuts, bruises or sunburns. Our success led us to acquire a small boat with a big outboard motor and a trailer, which we hauled on several camping expeditions. Our favorite sites were the state park at Clear Lake in northern California and Frank's Tract Lake in the Sacramento River delta. Charles and Ginny became quite accomplished water skiers. I actually managed to get up on two skis. There were good times.

Raymonde did not take to the water skiing, but she did enjoy fast rides across the lake in the open boat. Camping she treated as a sort of necessary evil, to be accommodated as little as possible. The rest of the family never forgot the sight of her in a line for the ladies' shower facility. There were these ladies in sweat-suits, rough pullovers, bare feet or flaps; and there was Raymonde, in a flowered pink silk bathrobe and gold slippers–she always went by her own style, and with class.

Progress in education picked up. Ginny went to the University of California at Los Angeles in September 1973 and graduated in June 1975 with a Bachelor of Arts degree, majoring in History. Raymonde and I went to her graduation exercises, held in a sports stadium. We also discovered that Ginny and Judy Schwarz, a high-school friend, had acquired a motorcycle on which they had happily buzzed around the UCLA area. It was enough to start grey hairs on their parents' heads. Back in Los Altos, Ginny went through some odd jobs–bank teller, sales clerk–then chose a career in the U.S. Navy. After being accepted at the Oakland Recruiting Station she went to Officer Candidate School in Newport, Rhode Island. It was a hard study–celestial navigation and ship's engineering especially–but she persevered and graduated in January 1978 as an Ensign, USNR. Raymonde and I went to Newport for the occasion and encountered there a snowstorm that buried cars under two feet of white stuff. It was quite a change from California.

Chuck progressed through a year at Northwestern Preparatory School in Minnesota, odd jobs and a period as a research assistant at Ames Research Center of the National Aeronautics and Space Agency. In August of 1981, he started studies at California State University at Long Beach, from which he graduated in May 1985 with Bachelor of Science degree in Mechanical Engineering. A large family gathering in Long Beach celebrated the event. He then took on work as an Engineer in the Civil Service at the USN Pacific Missile Test Center, Point Mugu. His interest in remote-controlled model airplanes helped him get the job. In his work he dealt with full-sized jet fighters, F4s for example, that were flown by remote control to serve as targets.

It's worth noting that Raymonde and I encouraged our children to complete their undergraduate education at distant universities, when they could have stayed close to home and studied at schools near Los Altos. This was a "sink-or-swim" process, but it was done on purpose. We considered that it was important for both children, with reasonable support, to get away from home and to learn to deal with society on their own terms. There were dangers, of course, but the risks seemed acceptable and things turned out well.

Thus, by 1985, both Ginny and Charles were well educated and had a good start on their careers. Raymonde and I enjoyed a quiet satisfaction with their achievements. With affection, modulated discipline and a strong sense of right and wrong, we had guided our children to strength and maturity. It wasn't easy. There had often been arguments, revolts, resentment and opposition. Their childhood had coincided with turbulent times and powerful social trends. We were all fortunate in that the two young ones avoided the "flower children," the "hippie lifestyle," the "dirty speech" movement, the "do-your-own-thing" philosophy and drug addiction. They came through the time successfully due to their parents' attention and their own common sense.

Family education did not end with the children. Raymonde had always resented the failure of U.S. agencies to recognize her European nursing credentials. Of course, when the children were young, most of her time was occupied; on one listing of work experience she described her work from 1957 to 1970 as "Mother's duties." Now, though, she could look to her own career. In June 1971, she took the examination and won her certification as a Registered X-ray Technologist in the state of California. After part-time work at the Mountain View Clinic, during which she met Adele Porcello, a very good friend, she did volunteer work in the spring of 1972 at the Palo Alto Veteran's Administration Hospital. This was rewarded with a certificate of outstanding volunteer services (500 hours) at the hospital.

In June 1972, with her confidence renewed and her ambition excited, Raymonde decided to launch into a program of nursing studies at De Anza, a local community college. "I have to regain my intellectual discipline, which I have neglected these past few years," she said. The courses included biology and microbiology. Anatomy and Physiology was a real challenge–I remember her coming home and using rather unladylike language to describe the instructor. Also, as one of the oldest in the class, she did not mingle well with some of the other students. There were a few group social functions; at one, Raymonde and I were happily surprised to be told by the young students, "You are a lovely couple," on the dance floor. The program was strenuous, but in September 1974, she completed the course for Licensed Vocational Nurses. She took and passed the California Board examination and received her LVN state license. Then she undertook part-time work in nursing at convalescent hospitals and skilled-nursing facilities–the University Branch in Menlo Park, Casa Olga in Palo Alto, etc. It was not easy, but it had its diversions; one day she returned from her shift with a big grin. An old fellow had escaped from Casa Olga and was contentedly roaming the streets when the police rounded him up–a major sensation! Later, from 1989 to 1991, Raymonde worked as the LVN technician giving treadmill tests in the Cardiology Department, Sunnyvale Medical Clinic. A clinic personnel evaluation commended her: "Raymonde has a definite talent for alleviating the anxiety of her patients."

During this period in her career, Raymonde was diagnosed with tuberculosis. She was immediately concerned about the danger of transmission to others. Fortunately, though, she went to the public service facility at Valley Medical Center and found a competent, sympathetic physician who prescribed proper medication that cleared her lungs. She got quick, effective treatment and moral support.

Homemaking and part-time nursing not being enough to absorb her energies, Raymonde joined and did work for the Republican Party. A life of overcoming difficulties had made Raymonde a strong woman, strengthening her political beliefs as well. She was a fervent political conservative. She had friends like Marcella McDonald to work with; they became delegates for Barry Goldwater at a convention at the Cow Palace in San Francisco. Later, as a reward for her party activity, she received a certificate of "Special Recognition" on the 20 January 1981 occasion of the inauguration of Ronald Reagan as the 40th president of the United States. He was "her president." The inauguration postal envelope is a family treasure.

Ginny's Navy career continued to advance. She went from training duty in San Diego through various assignments to administrative duty in Mayport, Florida. On an assignment in Washington, D.C., she met Lieutenant Matthew J. Streeter, USN. They fell in love, and on 1 October 1983, were married in a white-uniform Navy ceremony at the U.S. Naval Academy chapel in Annapolis, Maryland. Judy Schwarz and another good friend from high school, Suzie Thomas Kurtz, were bridesmaids; Matt's sister Maureen Ross was matron of honor. Chuck and Matt's brother Mark read portions of scripture. It was a high point in Raymonde's life and mine when the best man, Lieutenant Mike Reed USN, came to attention at the chapel doors and announced, "Ladies and Gentlemen, for the first time, I present Lieutenant and Mrs.

Matthew Streeter!" It was a major family gathering, including the reception on a sightseeing boat on the Potomac River. We gave Matt a special welcome; he is one of those persons for whom Raymonde developed particular affection and approval.

After a couple of relatively short-term assignments, Matthew and Ginny went to tours of duty in San Diego. It was here that, on 14 December 1984, in a flurry of excitement and strain, Zachary James Streeter came into the world. The delivery was a difficult one. Sister Maureen and friend Anne Ryan were on hand to comfort Ginny; Charles was called in from Long Beach and I from Los Altos to render moral support and feeble masculine assistance. The arrival of a healthy Zack was a great event for his grandparents.

Our twenty-eight years in Los Altos were a time of professional advancement, family development, social progress, financial success and loving. Opportunities came to us from several directions, and in particular there were chances to travel. The first joint trip for Raymonde and me was in 1962 to Lausanne, Bayonne, Normandy and Brussels. The expedition was something of a qualified success; it was fun but overly strenuous, showing that we had a lot to learn about traveling in Europe together. Nonetheless, it did let Raymonde revisit her early days—both the rough times and the good memories. In Villers-sur-Mer we visited Madame Cadoret, a long-time family friend; the good lady was not complimentary about the van Laars' decision to leave town when it was under reconstruction. At Lausanne we stayed with Aunt Madeleine and Uncle André Petitmaitre at Villa Florissant; she was still managing the pension, which had about forty residents. Madeleine was a well-groomed, handsome, accomplished lady of about sixty years. Andre was a long-term banker at Credit Suisse, a heavy-set man with an undershot jaw and a rather serious manner. They were fluent only in French. They both took to Raymonde with great affection. I was something of an enigma to them, but, being on good behavior, I was able to avoid any serious social blunders.

On an especially good day of this trip we took a jaunt from Lausanne to visit Gerzensee. We went by train via Berne to the "regional stop" at Wichtrach and on a 4-km hike to the van Laars' old estate. The village of Wichtrach is in the German-speaking region. It has just a tiny one-room railroad station. Raymonde, seeking directions, asked the lone stationmaster if he spoke French, to which he replied, "Ah, madame, ici nous parlons toutes les langues, aussi le francais." (Oh, madam, here we speak all the languages, even French). She was embarrassed.

It was September, the weather clear and cool with scattered clouds, a beautiful time in Switzerland. We walked up the hills from Wichtrach. Along the way, Raymonde could not resist the temptation to pat the cows in the fields near the fence at the road's edge. These beasts were a good ten times her size, but were "cute." Later we learned that a bus route had a regular run up the hill.

Gerzensee is a typical Swiss town of some thirty homes. There is a main street along which are located a chateau with a large yard, a modern building housing a school, barns with stables and equipment for stock and most of the houses of the town. Mature green trees are everywhere. A typical house has two-and-a-half stories, a peaked tile roof, and a ground-level garage. The upper two stories have white walls with brown exposed beams and green shutters on the windows. Geraniums in a riot of bloom spill out from large window boxes. In one of the two-story houses is located a restaurant with a porch at the back for open-air dining; at the time of our visit it served only the noon meal (dejeuner a midi = large lunch).

The estate that was once the van Laars' is located a short distance up the hill from the town center. The main house is two stories with a peaked third floor and brown shingle roof, and is surrounded by tall, shady trees. There is a courtyard out front and double porches framed in flowering vines.

We eventually arrived at the estate on foot and were met with an impressive sight. The view downhill from the estate captures the entirety of the town with its trees and red tile roofs. In every direction stretched trim, orderly fields, like vast green carpets. Our eyes ranged over the neat, flower-dotted graveyard of a small chapel, across small lakes and open fields with grazing cattle, to snow-covered mountains in the hazy distance.

The home of the estate was impressively well maintained and still owned by the Zaugg family. Hans Zaugg welcomed us in and let Raymonde visit her own old rooms on the second floor. When she told him how much she hated leaving Gerzensee, Mr. Zaugg said, "But you must forgive your father."

On these trips the variety of languages we encountered could be a problem. I struggled along with only a weak reading comprehension of French. I tried to persuade my wife to teach me, but she gave it up quickly; she could not bear to hear my "horrible accent."

Afterwards, about every other year, we made a trip to Switzerland. A favorite place for us to stay was the Hotel d'Angleterre in Ouchy close to the Petitmaitres' Villa Florissant. The hotel was a four-story structure of considerable age and classical architecture. The top floor was partly for staff lodging. There were no elevators. We usually were placed in a front room with a captivating view across the small-boat landing. The parks, street intersections and scenic walkways were brightened by flower plots maintained by city gardeners. On a clear day you could look out the window across the Lake of Geneva and see the French shore. At the hotel entrance was a wide patio opening onto the sidewalk and busy street intersection. We often enjoyed morning coffee and croissants there. Raymonde would occasionally be reprimanded by the waiter for tossing crumbs to the sparrows that flocked to any table that looked like a good source of provender.

Ginny had an enjoyable stay there on one trip with Ray. She had earlier been given a trip to Lausanne on a short course of instruction in French as a UCLA graduation present. She practiced her French on Niccola, the hotel maitre'd, to the laughter of both. On another visit, Charles was with us. The Hotel d'Angleterre gave him the front room in which Lord Byron resided while he wrote his poem "The Prisoner of Chillon."

When Uncle Andre retired, he and Madeleine moved to an apartment; they invited Raymonde to visit. She took advantage of the invitation. While there she wrote to me often:

September 24ᵗʰ, 1968

My Darling!
Since the plane has finally stopped to jump up and down like a Kangaroo (over Nebraska), I want to send you my love and my thoughts. My place was on the right of the plane so I couldn't wave at you all, but when it turned to take its place on the runway, I could see the three of you on the observation deck, and my heart broke out. I miss you all already, and Uncle Andre better be nice or I get back on the next flight home.

The flight on United was wonderful. It was not crowded at all. My next seat was free and the other one was occupied by a young man (married) fairly flat in his conversation so I have the time to read and write. As the planes are empty, I will ask Swissair if I can sit alone, so I will be able to stretch for the night, and they might do it.

From the window the weather is so-so, quite cloudy.

We had steak for lunch; I was a good girl, I ate only the meat, salad and pimiento. It was really good. I made the mistake of ordering a sherry before lunch (they were offering cocktails, yes sirree) and they gave me a dry sherry imported from England. Yak! I never tasted such vial beverage. I will never order it again. Enjoy your California sherry, it is really the best.

I love you, love you, love you so much and miss you so much already. Please hug the kids for me. I miss them too so much.

Be kind to Jezebel, happy in your work, and I adore you,

Raymonde

Next she sent:

September 27th, 1968

My very own darling,

I am having such a wonderful time here; what a difference from the last visit, it cannot be compared.

I do believe that when you apply independence it makes the point.

Yesterday we took the boat, Madeleine and I to St. Gingol which is the terminal of the "cruise" after passing Chateau of Chillon, and we went back same route, picking up Andre at Vevey. Andre spent the whole day at the chalet, watering, cutting the grass, and fooling around. It was his day, so I enjoyed Madeleine all by myself so much.

I went to town yesterday morning also, to buy paper, envelopes, stamps, etc., and look at windows, prices of clothes, etc. I do believe that I will take a day off from Madeleine and Andre to investigate everything with care before I decide.

Madeleine looks so much better since I came and I believe that I am taking her mind off a lot of unnecessary worries.

The weather is fair and cool, but the beauty of fall here is spectacular. The lake is so grey and calm, and it is full of swans.

The food here is delicious as usual, but in small quantities and we eat a lot of fresh fruits (no "Schlog") so don't you worry about my waistline.

Time is already going so fast but I miss you so much and I am so anxious to hear from you and know how you are all getting along. Be careful with the boat and

your driving. Oh darling, how wonderful you are to have let me go and have such a good time.
I hope I can make it for you when I come back.
I miss you, love you, adore you forever,

Raymonde

A special attraction, for both locals and tourists, on the Lake of Geneva (as on several European lakes) are the passenger boats operated by the Companie General de la Navigation. A boat typically follows a scheduled route that may stop at the landing of every town along some of the lake's shores, or it may go on a sightseeing cruise around the lake. When Raymonde writes of "going on the lake," she refers to such a voyage; she sometimes liked to call it "taking a trip on the Swiss Navy." The more modern boats are stylish, diesel-powered double-deckers. The boats of earlier vintage are long and narrow with a handsome sweep to the main deck, restaurant on the main and benches for on-lookers on the upper deck. Some have been converted to diesel power. Over the course of our visits at least one, the *Italie,* had a fully operational reciprocating-engine steam plant driving side-mounted paddle wheels. For anyone who appreciated fine early machinery it was a delight to see. The officers and crew operated with typical Swiss efficiency. Schedules were kept to the minute, except on at least one occasion when the landing had to be delayed so that a mother swan and her new brood could swim out of the way. Raymonde claimed that damage to a swan would be enough to wreck a pilot's reputation.

Next, from this 1968 trip, she wrote:

September 30ᵗʰ, 1968

My very own Darling,
Almost a week since I left, and it seems like a century. I do believe that I will write in an English more awful than usual. I speak too much French here.

In spite of a lot of rain, we have already done so much: saw the Pleiades, and twice on the lake, one over the Chateau de Chillon, the other to Nyon.

Saturday afternoon it was raining so I went to town by myself and window-shopped at Place St. Francois. It was fun. I found a confiserie and sent seven boxes of chocolates, including for you. I would like to have the Morris house number as I like to send them one also.

I looked at the price of dressy watches. They are lovely and the price reasonable compared to the U.S. A super deluxe one, first price, all in 18 carat gold, including the bracelet, 350 Fr to up to 6 or 700 Fr, but the ones between 350 and 400, which is around 85 to 90 dollars, are very pretty and very chic in design. Then you have the watch all gold (18 carats) with suede bracelet for 250, 200, etc.

I am afraid that the price of gold in Switzerland remains very reasonable, so the American investors better think twice about their quicky way of making money with this metal.

This morning, Monday, the shops are closed, so I am going to the hairdresser; this afternoon my aunt has her bridge lesson and Andre will take me at Ouchy to show me the place of their Exposition of 64, which the Swiss are still talking about.

The evenings we watch TV and the news are very accurate. Poor Humphrey, he has a very poor press here and they give him 1 out of 7 chances to be President.

I am heartbroken of course.

Just came back from town and found your letter, my darling, and the one from Charles. How very sweet from both of you. Oh! If you would know how I miss you all. No, I won't stay another day after the 15th. Only two more weeks and I am back.

Tomorrow I believe I will start to go shopping for the children. I do believe that I am familiar enough to the prices here. I hope I will have luck.

I am having a wonderful time, and Andre and Madeleine do not know what to do to please me. Andre gave me 2 envelopes of stamps plus a catalogue of Swiss stamps; I do have some good values, glancing at some of the issues I have. I went to the hairdresser this morning and a wash and set cost $2.50 including tips. Quite a difference.

Please take good care of yourself and hug the kids for me. Be kind to the pussy-cats. I miss Jezebel and Kitchi-Kou. I am sure they are perched on the trees and don't dare come down.

I wonder how your project is going in Arizona.

I have to go now. I love you and miss you and adore you. Give my love to the kids. Thank you for this lovely vacation; you are a saint.

Remember we have a date Oct. 18th in S.F.

Forever yours,
Raymonde

Andre took Madeleine and Raymonde to Lugano in the Italian-Swiss region for a couple days' excursion. At this time, I was on a business trip to Fort Huachuca, Arizona, where I received the following letter. Note that Ray's translation from Spanish to French to English gave her writing its own distinctive flavor.

October 6th, 1968

My Darling,
We are leaving this morning Lugano. It was a lovely vacation. Yesterday we went to visit the little town of Gandria. Typically Italian, the little church is a pure wonder, all walls and ceiling artistically painted. I would say, almost like the Cystine Chapel of Rome. As a conservative, you can imagine my delight.
I am glad to come back to Lausanne where I will be able to get your mail. It seems to me that it was ages since I have heard from you.
The weather keeps being beautiful. We are so lucky.
I wonder how you are all. Are you going boating these days? How is Fort "Watchouka" getting along?
I wonder how Dawson found SRI after a year of absence! I will send them a card from Lausanne as I don't have my address book with me.
Andre and Madeleine think I do too much politics because I stood up to Andre yesterday, as Andre took part for the Russians for not letting reunite Germany. It is terrific to see the ignorance of the Swiss and how they can support the Russians instead of the Germans is unbelievable. So, I shall not discuss politics anymore, as our relations otherwise are most harmonious.

I love you, miss you and adore you. My love to the children. By now, Ginny must be an accomplished cook...!

I adore you as ever,
Raymonde

She often wrote of her pleasure in receiving letters from me and Ginny and Chuck. The next-to-last letter from this trip was:

October 8th, 1968

My Darling,
A week from today, I am taking the plane back home. How wonderful. I would have had a most delightful time here and the memory of it will be long to cherish.
Yesterday the weather was just delightful in Lausanne and as Aunt Madeleine went for her bridge lessons, I went on the Quay d'Ouchy and strolled along by myself in places full of memories of my past. It was lovely and strange at the same time, like a stranger looking at a dream long past. I bought a large loaf of bread and went to feed the swans, "sea gulls" and little water hens. By the time I finished I had all the birds of Ouchy eating at my hands, a crowd of children perfectly happy to see the show, and gentlemen taking pictures as they had never seen so many swans and other birds in one place. Stupidly, I didn't have my camera with me, so couldn't take a picture. But I shall repeat my performance before I go.
I found two French grammar books, and today I

111

sent by mail 5 books and a bunch of chocolats given by Madeleine, by the post-office. I have to watch my weight, and I thought that was a good idea. I am afraid, I won't bring much money home, but bought lovely things for all of us.

Tonight we are going out to dinner with the family of George Clemenceau, grandson of the late "Tiger" of 1st World War. It will be interesting.

Tomorrow night, Andre took tickets for the Circus Knie. Things are looking up mighty busy and wonderful.

I am so happy to think that less than a week I will be home. I love you and miss you and I am forever yours,

Raymonde

The camping week-end is over. I hope you are all home safe and sound.

On the evening of October 15th, she arrived back at San Francisco to the joyous welcome of all three members of her family. As she said, "My vacations were a complete success; I am so rested and happy."

Raymonde and I celebrated her return four days later with dinner at the Fairmont Hotel of San Francisco.

After this, about every second year, Ray made repeats of her visit to her aunt and uncle in Pully, a town on the outskirts of Lausanne. In the early 1970's, Europe was having trouble making the Common Market work; the different countries experienced difficulties with currency control. Italy, for example, let its lira debase in order to pay for social benefits. The strongest were the German mark and the Swiss franc, and even these two got into arguments over relative values. Financial affairs and monetary practices fluctuated so widely and so often that the rates of exchange with U.S. dollars, which came as close as any to being an international standard, could not be predicted with certainty. This situation was resolved a few years later with the formation of the European Union and the introduction of the euro.

During a trip in 1971, Raymonde went one day with Madeleine to her bridge class and reported proudly that she "made a hit, got along well with all these ladies, and in all modesty won almost all the hands." Later she ran into money exchange difficulties and wrote:

May 6ᵗʰ, 1971

Mon amour cherie!
Two letters of you, yesterday and today, also a letter of each of my precious children. Oh! How I wish you would be all with me.
After two days of uncertain weather, today was a glorious day, warm, sunny.
Before I go back on my activities, let me tell you how much I needed your lovely letters, your love and all. I was quite depressed yesterday after spending all afternoon with Jeannine at Aigle. She is so terribly unhappy and works so hard to try to get some extra money for herself. I saw her husband who is nice but as stupid as three big flat feet (whatever that is) and he does't give her a penny for her clothes or else. Naturally Jeannine forgets how she behaved with him in the past, but I can't but have pitty when someone is

down. When I came back, the news of the dollar were not to cheer me up. I can't change any travellers check till there is a settlement with the Mark. If I have to change (20 or 40 dollars) it is at 3.80 instead of 4.27. So Andre advised me to wait till Monday to see where the situation will be.

However, without saying anything, I will go early tomorrow morning to Ouchy at the little exchange place that I know and try to change or ask him if I can buy French francs with my dollars, then convert these French francs in Swiss ones. I don't think I would loose much.

I cancelled my trip to France as I don't want to be stuck there if they stop changing American dollars. What a mess, but it was to be expected. I do hope it won't alter your trip. I miss you so, so very much. I can't wait to see you.

Madeleine and Andre are just darlings. I have been on the lake already twice and especially today it was gorgeous. Tomorrow at noon we are going to eat a fondue with their cousins at la "Tour de Peilz." They live near Vevey and, according to Andre, have a lovely apartement.

Andre is very nervous with the dollar situation as he has some actions paid in dollars. I still think that it will settle soon, but in the meantime it is't funny.

I am so grateful to be with Madeleine and Andre and not worry about food and roof, but I hope it won't be long before I can be independent again. What is the reaction in the U.S? I was wondering how you will manage in Germany with your travellers checks in dollars. I will try to change as much as I can here to the best I can, so I can "support" you when you come *to see me. I would love you to take Madeleine and Andre out for dinner, and maybe you and I can go to Zermatt one day.*

In the meantime I have to be very careful with my spending. I have sent 12 boxes of chocolat to friends but that was extravagant and was done before the dollar got stuck. I still have 600 dollars, I changed a 100, regular change the day before it stopped. If I would have known I would have changed everything because I can't loose changing it back to dollars. Oh! Well, everything else is so perfect, and I am so, so grateful to be able to have some rest, and so, so grateful that you are so generous and understanding.

Oh! I miss you so much. You are a darling to have paid the house and utilities, also to have put all the check in the checking account. Please do the same the 14th. When I come back we will switch back to the saving account.

Donc forget to take the check book with you and take or hide the saving books. Thank you for the address of Mrs. Caspari.

I love you, love you, love you and bless the Lord to have married you. European men are impossible!

You are so perfect and lovely. When ever I have been nasty to you, I should have "crocked" on the spot.

Please hug the kids for me. I miss them so much and I am so proud of them. I love them so. They wrote so nicely.

I send you all my dearest love. For ever yours,

Raymonde

May 7th, 1971

My very own Darling!
What a day. This Friday morning in the newspapers, it was announced that banks were changing dollars again but at reduced rates.

I had very little time to make my steps as Andre left the house at 9 am for some secret errands; Madeleine had to leave at 9 also to go to her doctor and we all made a date at the station at 11:45 to take the train to go to eat a fondue at Vevey with famous cousins.

I had to wait till 9:30 to leave Madeleine's apartment so her maid could get in. She finally came so I was able to take the bus at 10am. At Place St. Francois I went to all the banks I could think of and they all turned me down and suggest that I go to the office of American Express. After going up and down streets I finally found the d... office and they were willing to accept my dollars at 4.10 instead of 4.26. Well it was 16 Swiss cents less but I went ahead and changed all my 500 dollars. So I have now 2050 Swiss francs plus the 427 Swiss francs that I changed at the beginning of the week. In all I lost about 83 Swiss francs but I think I did well.

The situation here is a mess! There is little hope that the Germans will agree with the six other nations, so I don't know what will happen Monday but I don't think I did wrong. Anyway I am going to be very careful with everything and wait for you to come then shop for the children.

I didn't say anything to Andre yet. I want to see what the change if any will be Monday. As always, Andre didn't offer any help for a solution. Strange man. He loves me very much, I think, but when it comes to reassure me, I can only find the word "reassurance" in the dictionary.

I was wondering that when you go to Nuremberg, I would like to join you there around the 24th or 25th (I am invited at the Tour de Peilz for the cousin Kurz 86 springs and they are really nice). I miss you so, so much.

So this is the state of affairs. It is much more serious and is not printed in the newspapers or if it is, it is treated very lightly. Anyway I am happy to have this worry over and I can only gain because if the dollar goes down, when I will change back the rest of my Swiss francs, going home I will gain more dollars.

But let me tell you, it isn't funny to think that your money is worth something and the banks turn you flat down.

I wonder if you have written your letter about the patent situation. I hope so, the sooner the better.

I am so sorry you had a bad case of hay-fever. Pretty soon it will be over, I hope, and we can enjoy the summer.

The trip to Vevey today was very nice. The cousins of Andre, charming and very hospitable. They have a beautiful apartment with a gorgeous view on the lake and mountains. It was also a lovely day. But I came home very tired, I don't know why.

In spite of all these going out and eating well, my weight is 51 kg or 111 lbs so don't worry I am not fat. Maybe it is because I miss you so much.

Please take good care of yourself I love you, love you, love you.

Kiss the kids for me. I miss them so much too...

For ever yours,
Raymonde

P.S. Try to have your travelers check American
Express because you can go to their office if the banks
refuse your checks. At least there is a little support
there.

The patent Raymonde referred to here was an
application for an idea I had about a medical instrument;
it did not work out.

On a business trip to Germany, I met Ray in
Nuremberg. After my work was completed we "played
tourists," strolling the Medieval streets, admiring the
reconstruction after war damage, having dinner at
the Heiligeispital, and taking in Beethoven's opera
Fidelio.

Trips to Switzerland were not only opportunities to
renew our acquaintance with Aunt Madeleine, Uncle
Andre, and cousins Jeannine Auckenthaler Blanchut
and Eric Auckenthaler. They also gave Raymonde a
chance to renew contact with her roots, to have a change
from California life, and to re-stoke her energy. They
offered amusement at times. On one evening at the
Petitmaitre chalet in Villars, Andre declared it a special
occasion and opened a valuable bottle of wine he had
been hoarding. He bragged, "The dust is still on the
bottle." Raymonde said later that it tasted "just awful,"
but she apparently didn't confess that to Andre.

A trip in 1975 evoked memories of previous visits
and concerns. Andre and Madeleine had met Ginny
when she visited earlier. Aunt Madeleine's health was
a cause of worry to everyone in the family.

September 11ᵗʰ, 1975

Mon amour cheri!
It is only now that I can go to the Post Office and send you a night letter. I take this opportunity to mail this letter also, written early this morning. My trip went fine all along the way, all time taken, 12 hours from San Francisco to Geneva plus 2 hours wait in New York. The service in T.W.A was perfect, however, I didn't get the seats I was told I would have when I made my reservation. Going to New York I was near the window, but had a very nice young girl beside me. From New York I had the middle seat, which I detest, between 2 gentlemen who were very courteous and gallant, so that made up for the discomfort.

However, I couldn't close my eyes, so after dinner I watch the movie "Never on Sunday," which I thought was totally "Blah!!!." But right after, breakfast was served and we arrived shortly in Geneva, ½ hour early. Practically no custom action, passeport no problem. I had the time to freshen up, and sat patiently at the place where Andre told me to wait for him, and he was there shortly after, absolutely delightful. We had a "coffe crème" and took the train to Lausanne. The weather was kind of hot and muggy, but everythink looked beautiful.

I have a lovely room at Montillier, much better than 2 years ago. Already went on the lake, same afternoon because Andre was afraid of a coming storm, so he wanted to take advantage of the sun. It was just lovely. Went to Vevey and back. I did't feel tired at all. I am so happy. Madeleine gave me a beautiful gift:

the Petitmaitre family blazon on solid gold ring. It is perfectly beautiful and so sweet of Madeleine to have thought of it. She has one the same, thought she has lost it, made another one, then found the original, so had two and shared them with me. It is so simple, chic and beautiful.

Today we are going to a small town on the French coast, reputed for its beauty. All day on the lake, I am looking forward to it. The rest of the week, the Comptoir Swiss is open, and I will visit it. I do know that my stay will be short but so very lovely. I am so glad I came. Andre and Madeleine still talked about their pleasure to know Ginny and how she was so charming, and lovely, and delightful. Do we have a daughter of that name? Ha! Also the picture of Charles made a fantastic impression. He is so "manly" looking and good looking. Well all in all I was quite proud of my little family.

Andre predict a fantastic storm today, but it is his style: between the train, boat and weather predictions, it is a busy career. He will get me some new stamps today also.

Hope all is well on the California's front. Time is going so fast, I will be back before I know it.

I miss you all.

Hope Ginny got a card written from the chalet by Madeleine and Andre. I know a little note in French from her to them will please them so very much. I gave them your loving message of thanks for doing so much with Ginny.

I think of you and adore you. Dearest love and kisses to the kids.

As always,
Raymonde

September 18th, 1975

Wade, my darling!
This is the last letter before I take my flight back to the U.S. My stay has both been long and short. Long because I miss you so much, short, because in spite of the rain, the schedule has been heavy.

Finally the weather has decided to be stable. So yesterday we went to Ivoire, a small medieval city, absolutely exquisite. We had dinner there, then visited the town. The weather was lovely, the boat ride perfect. Today I shall go the morning to Ouchy and feed the swans, then this afternoon we will go to the Comptoir Suisse. I do hope it won't be too much for Madeleine; she has suffered lately of dizziness and does't look too well.

Tomorrow we shall meet the Kurz at Vevey and have lunch with them; Saturday we are going to Gruyere which is also another medieval town. They make cheese also. Ha! Anyway it will be quite interesting and busy. Sunday, we'll collapse, Monday, last run for shopping, Tuesday back to the U.S.

It has been a lovely vacation, but my emotions run always very high. Oh yes, I will try to contact Mme. Giovanola Monday, and see if I can meet her. I would love to.

Andre is always bossy, busy (anyway acting like it) and most of the time charming. Excitement! Yesterday, he bought 100 bottles of wine through the Club Alpin and I do believe he was up since 4am to not miss the meeting with his friend. I am looking for a bottle of Fondant du Valais, it is't easy to find, but I will, I will.

Hope you are all well and both cars still running and together. Also, I do believe you are in a trip or back from it, and I do hope it was all perfect.

I am still so very proud of your paper been accepted. What an accomplishment. I am so very proud of you.

Please give my love to Ginny and Charles. A pat to Jezzi-Poo.

To you I send my dearest love as always and my special thoughts...

As ever,
Raymonde

Madeleine and Andre send their love to all.

She made several such trips by herself, and took me along on a couple. I once suggested that we choose some other places to visit—Athens, for example, to see the Parthenon. "Every educated Western person should contemplate this temple of Greek civilization at least once in his life," I told Raymonde. Raymonde's answer was that if she had to fly ten thousand miles she wanted to land in a civilized place.

When the children were young, we would hire a house sitter to stay with them during these trips. Our experiences with these ladies were uniformly good. When Ray went alone, I tended the home and looked out for the kids. It usually worked out all right except that my culinary expertise did not extend far beyond breakfast; when it came to dinner I made mistakes, like too much spice in a stew, which required intervention in the kitchen by the kids. Chuck and Ginny did not seem to suffer too much. In one letter Raymonde remarked, "I know Ginny is a jewel in the house, replacing me for most everything." She had confidence that her family could avoid big catastrophes.

In June 1978, Aunt Madeleine had a mild heart attack that put her in the hospital. At Andre's urging, Raymonde went to Switzerland:

Lausanne September 7th, 1978

My darling,

Finally I can settle down at the hairdresser today, as I decided to keep my weekly schedule like at home, and write you a note.

I had a marvelous trip on Swissair, arrived in Geneva at 7am and was at my hotel at 8:15am, a record.

I did not get my usual room as they made a mistake but I ended to have for the same price a much better one on the 3rd floor, no noise, just a pure marvel.

The weather was rain all the way but it was so hot and heavy when I came the rain is a blessing and is cooling down everything.

Now, I found Madeleine not as bad off as I expected... She is awfully thin and her posture has slump down a lot. This, I think, is a sign of her age which is very apparent. However, it seems that since I came back, she has perked up and looks better. She is always very groomed and well dressed, which helps.

Her doctor came last night and was very pleased, but he is very stricked and wants her to stick to the same routine, rest and relaxation and no stairs.

Yesterday, in spite of the rain, Andre and I took the boat to Montreux and back. This gave Madeleine the time to sleep all afternoon, so that was good.

Today as you know I went to the hairdresser at 8am, then will take the train to Aigle to see Jeaninne who is off today. So I wont see Madeleine but tonite.

The Comptoir Suisse opens Saturday and Jeaninne, her friend Lize and I are planning an escape for a whole day. Andre also has tickets for this occasion so we will go together and spend other days there.

Saturday also Madeleine will go to her hairdresser and then we will have lunch at a restaurant near the lake at Pully.

Andre looks very well. Complains about his knee and back and so forth. I noticed that the complains are more loud when Madeleine is better, so to get some attention. You, Men!!!

The change is a disaster. When I landed Tuesday, the dollar was at 1.54, now is back to 1.60. I am extatic!! I am glad I took all these travellers checks, but I do watch very carefully any expenses I may make. Anyway, I am sure I will survive very nicely

In spite of the rain and the change, I am having a lovely time and Madeleine and Andre are just darlings.

I think of you my darling all the time and I miss you and love you. Say hello to Charles, hope he continues his flights with great success.

To both of you, all my love,
Raymonde

And next:

September 8th, 1978

Darling Wade
First let me tell you how wonderful it was to read
your sweet letter. It came two days ago and see only
now I can tell you how much I love you.
Terrible!!!
First I got your letter when I came back from visiting
Jeaninne all day last Thursday. We had a lovely time.
Had lunch at her place, then we took a stroll into the
town of Aigle which is really lovely, old and charming.
Unfortunately it was raining all day so we had to cut
short our walk and could't make it to the Chateau of
Aigle. We made a date with Jeaninne and Lise next
Wednesday or Thursday at the Comptoir Suisse. We
will have a ball.

Yesterday, Hurrah! The sun is here so after
wandering at Place St. Francois and mailing cards I
had written to my friends, went back to Madeleine's
place, had lunch then went with Mr. Monnier, the
minister who married Andre and Madeleine and who
is a close friend of the family, for a ride in the country
side in his car, with Andre also.

Mr. Monnier is widowed from June 77 and is about
to marry a distant cousin 12 years his junior because
he is fed up to do his cooking, laundry, cleaning and be
alone. So, as you see my darling, widowers do not last
long in my native country.

I do not know how long this letter will take. I wrote
you the 6th so you should get it next week. Also I sent
you a night letter to tell you about my safe landing.

Madeleine is holding her own but I wonder at time. The doctor is coming back Monday evening, so we'll see.

I wrote Ginny yesterday. She sent two cards to Andre and Madeleine from St. Augustine, Florida, written in French and really not bad at all. Andre wrote her back recently after I gave him for the second time her address. You, Men!!!

Otherwise I am resting a lot and reading at night some fantastic books Madeleine lent me, written by Philippe Bouvard, about sarcasm in politics and journalism. It is written in a beautiful and witty French and so much to the point. It is fascinating. Read the first book in 2 days and nights. Started the 2nd one this morning and had to leave it, first to write you, then to meet Andre and Madeleine to a restaurant at Pully for lunch. I like to see how we will get back Madeleine to her appartement "without stairs!!!"

So, for now, so long my Darling, I love you and miss you and sends you tons of love'

Raymonde

Madeleine died suddenly in December of 1978 and Andre went into a depression. After affairs were put in order, Raymonde traveled to Pully to be of moral support and comfort to Andre. Agathe Colliard was the Petitmaitre maid; the Schneiders were their landlords.

May 8ᵗʰ, 1979

Darling
Can't believe that I have been 3 days here. Coming

on Saturday handicapped a lot of my plans as to send you a wire to tell you I have well arrived.

The trip was good except that the amount of kids on plane really makes the voyage very challenging even on Swissair. Two letters full of "friendly suggestions" will be going to both airlines for further references.

Anyway I arrived on Saturday morning with rain snow (yes SNOW) and a cold weather to please all the polar bears in the world. It took one day to get the cold wind out, the rain and snow to stop, and today (as yesterday) the weather has been gorgeous. I am becoming a legend to bring good weather to my native Switzerland.

Andre is well, better than I thought, but the loss of Madeleine and I suppose his age show on him. He does not "galopped" the way he used too with Madeleine. He even wait without swearing for the red lights to change. Oh! I wish so much, Madeleine would have known such a restrain in him.

My emotions run very strong as I always expect Madeleine to walk right into the appartement. As I did not see her dead, her loving souvenir is so vivid. Maybe it is best. Andre is very happy with my visit but breaks down often when he talks of Madeleine.

We have gone twice to the restaurant of Pully, once on the boat. Today the Monnier are coming to take us for a ride. He is the minister who married Andre and Madeleine. He remarried last year that dame who can cook and clean but who can stop a freight train on a downhill run with her appearance. I am just terrible as she is very nice and anxious to meet me.

Andre has made reservations for Lugano for next Sunday and we plan to stay about 5 days there. Agathe *goes on vacation tomorrow for 10 days I think.*

Yesterday afternoon I went shopping for a few things I needed it and found all what I wanted it.

The change is 1.69 so really not bad. I am glad I went at a time when Carter is not planning any future goofs (we hope). However, life here is horribly expensive and it is much cheaper in the U.S.

Agathe is well and has't changed. I also saw Mrs. And Mr. Schneider. They were very nice and are so pleased that I came for my visit. As a matter of fact Andre talked about me to all, just stopped to the President of Helvetia. I feel very flattered that I have such a big place in his life, but being very closed to Madeleine all these years, makes me close to him more now.

He is much less bossy too. My Gosh, never thought I would see that day to come.

There is something beautiful and sad at the same time to see how the loss of someone so dear, makes the one who is left, practically so helpless. So far he has some good friends and that help.

However last night he was talking to a friend Mr. Sleizag and this friend had a cousin, Andre met three weeks ago, who had just bought an appartement. Well that cousin dropped dead yesterday morning, so that shook up Andre a lot.

Otherwise I shall enjoy as much as I can my stay here. Seems like I will be quite busy visiting and travelling.

Give my love to Charles, and for you all my dearest love and kisses,

Raymonde

Two days later she replied to a letter of Chuck's; Ginny was now at her active Navy duty station in Florida. At this time, a series of events in the Middle East contributed to a gas shortage in the U.S. Many citizens thought the Carter administration handled the situation poorly, Raymonde included. Service stations had lines of vehicles extending for city blocks; some customers waited in line for several hours, only to find the pumps empty when they reached the station. Supplies became available after about a week, but the frustrations left their mark in the news.

Le 10 Mai 1979

Dear Charles.

Coming home yesterday from Gruyere, I found your letter and I was so pleased.

It was sweet of you to take the time to write me and to tell me such wonderful things.

Frankly I have been so busy, I have't had the time to think of home much, but I miss my two men regardless.

I had a very good trip on the plane except for the bratts, they take and put them everywhere to be sure we are all entertained.

Otherwise things went along pretty well and Swiss Air is really very organized and disciplined.

We are having a gorgeous weather and so far have been visiting Morat, near the Lake of Neuchatel, and the Roman ruins near Avenche just before Morat. It was most interesting, and we had a friend of Andre, Mr. Monnier, who is a retired minister and knows his Roman and Greek history like a book. My ears are still full of the rise and fall of the Roman Empire.

Sunday we'll go to Lugano and stay 4 to 5 days. After that it will be more like getting ready to go home again. Brace yourself the mean wench will be back.

I wonder if you will have your pilote license by the time I come back.

I also wonder about the gazoline situation. The news through the radio and papers here are pretty bad.

Here it is a joke as gazoline is plentiful all over the place. They can't understand that America with all its resources is crippled so stupidely for gaz. Oh well they don't know the Carter administration very well.

I hope you treat Jesabel well. Don't forget to change her water. It is important as she needs fresh water for her beauty and happiness.

I wonder about so many things concerning you. Regardless of my attitude, I am concerned about you and I love you very much.

Andre sends his best. He is so happy that I have come.

The weather is absolutely gorgeous, I am so lucky.

There are many military maneuvers here and the best ones are the jet planes. They got 150 jet 15 (?) from the USA and they could compete with the Blue Angels.

Hope all stays well with you two.

Think of you, Charles, and send you all my love, Mamy

Raymonde's visits to Switzerland were usually happy with just enough travel jolts and contact with contentious relatives to provide spice. On this trip, however, the loss of Aunt Madeleine cast a gloom over all her family. There were no elegant dinners in situations with beautiful views. Uncle Andre was naturally saddened and he withdrew into his own private world of grief. While Raymonde did her best to comfort him, the sense of distress weighed heavily on her and she also had to worry about Andre's future care. This all produced a major case of the blues; she became depressed and unhappy, in great contrast to her customary bright outlook on life.

May 12ᵗʰ, 1979

My Darling!
I don't know when you will receive this letter as the Mail is so slow getting to the U.S.
I received your letter yesterday the 3ʳᵈ one and it was lovely to read it. You are a very sweet husband and write so nicely.
Lately before I came here, I have had some very serious thoughts about my future. Life, really is't important, it is the quality of life which is. As far as I am concerned I have lived like a student all my life, messy house, demanding kids, most intellectual husband.
When I was young I could take it well as there was always hope. Now it is different. I see things much closer and as it looks, the future does't hold much for me to look forward. Oh! Don't worry, I shall carry on with a happy façade, but I cannot predict how long it will be.
Madeleine used to always give me courage, but she had much more security at my present age than

I have. Though she lived a much easier time in a well organized country which would never take as much "bullshit" that we take in America.

But now that she is gone, I feel suddenly very helpless and very old, and things don't matter with me or for me anymore.

We are leaving for Lugano tomorrow for a few days. Andre wants a pilgrimage in Madeleine's memory, so be it.

We will be at the Arizona hotel (which I detest), as I have told you before, it must have been an American Architect who flunked his tests in America, and somehow convinced Lugano that he was an original, but O.K.

I sent Ginny by airmail 2 boxes of chocolat. I am sure she will like them. I still have tons of cards to write. I can do it in Lugano, it will kill the time.

Life is terribly expensive here, and I don't know how Andre manage so well. He is very lucky to keep up his life style, but takes everything for granted.

The 22nd will be the grand tour with the Alpin Club. I think it will be lovely. We will go into "Central Switzerland." The group is lovely, they are all so myope (French for 'short-sighted') and they think I look so young. They always make my day.

Have you had other estimates for the door-window in the family room?

I read with terror the problem about gazoline. Really it is't necessary, but I guess we will all be paying the price of it.

Darling, thank you for writing me so often. Hope all is well.

I send you my love to you and Charles.

*I can say that I am flying back a week from Friday.
Will send you the time and flight tomorrow as I am
writing at the hairdresser.*
*I thought I left a copy of my schedule on top of your
dresser.*

All my love, always,
Raymonde

This letter shocked and scared me. I had never before
known my darling wife to have her spirits at such low
ebb. I wrote back quickly with an air of confidence and
the expression of my great love for her.

The visit to Lugano with Andre to "relive" their
memories of Madeleine did a lot to improve Andre's
morale and to relieve Raymonde's worries about his
health. Afterwards, Raymonde was ready to face the
U.S. again:

May 19th, 1979

Darling!
*Just back yesterday from Lugano and found your
sweet letters waiting for me. Also your anniversary
card. I really wept as I never thought I meant that
much to you.*
*Happy Anniversary, Darling, and I take a rain
check with you to celebrate when I come back.*
*I am starting again to sleep well, as in Lausanne
I have my mornings so I can sleep late. Hurrah.
Tomorrow Sunday we will see Christianne, Monday
I will go to Cook to reconfirm my return on Friday.*

Tuesday the Club Alpin is having his tour so I am included and I will love it I know.

Wednesday I made a date with Jeannine and perhaps Lise so we will have lunch at la "Residence" (old Florissant). I am looking forward to see her. I called her as soon as I came back from Lugano and she sounded lovely over the phone. Hope it lasts. Ha!

Today we had a lovely lunch at Pully then went to visit Sauvabelin which is above the lake of Lausanne. The weather was mixed but the sun shone while we were there. I always love Sauvabelin as Madeleine and I went so often just to talk and relaxe. She was with us every moment that afternoon and I loved it.

I am sending by boat a big parcel with a few things I thought I might be able to use and enjoy at home. It is too heavy in my suit cases, though I am bringing some lovely binded books done by Madeleine. I know you will appreciate them as much as I will. They are priceless.

Andre is very sad at the thought that I am leaving next Friday. He has been absolutely a darling in every way, though a handful at times but I understand his attitude. He feels so lonely and let down since Madeleine left. It is not funny to stay alone after being so happy for so many years.

I am glad we can still have some gazoline though it is difficult. I think that my coming on the 25th will be hard to get as it will be the end of the month and a hollyday weekend. Our great President is predicting an easier time in June... Ha!

Darling I love you very very much and I thank you for all the lovely messages you sent me. Sorry I was not as good as you.

See you soon. Hope you got my letter with the time of my arrival. Will call you from New York.

All my dearest love and kisses as always,
Ray
Love to Charles

After a lengthy illness involving a stay in a rest home, Andre died in April 1981. His affairs during this period were handled by Henri Sielaz, a lawyer and family friend. Raymonde traveled to Switzerland and acted as executor of the Petitmaitre estate. It was a demanding and emotionally difficult task, which she discharged carefully and conscientiously.

Thus the years in Los Altos passed, bringing both joyous events and doleful trials to be dealt with. Ray and I were deeply in love. We did not "grow old gracefully," but we always had each other for support and affection. Ginny and Chuck were sometimes challenging but have always been sources of love and pride.

By 1989 the kids were on their own and well established. Raymonde and I grew tired of gardening and yard work and decided to move to quarters with easier maintenance. We sold the house on E. Edith Street and, on 26 January 1990, moved to a place in the nearby city of Los Gatos.

7

RINCONADA HILLS

The complex called Rinconada Hills—in a highly corrupted Spanish—consisted of some 400 townhouses (one slice of a row of four or five units) and about 30 isolated family homes. It had a strong homeowners' association responsible for the exterior maintenance and appearance of the houses. Facilities included a clubhouse, a guarded gate, tennis courts, a club-sized swimming pool, and several "splashing pools" distributed around the clusters of houses. The area had easy hills, mature trees and shrubs, ponds and good walking trails. The circuit of the street that ran completely around the complex was advertised to be just one mile in length. Wildlife—squirrels, hummingbirds, ducks—were all around.

Raymonde and I bought 131 Callecita, a two-story unit in a row of five on a cul-de-sac street surrounded by three rows, making for a fair-sized section of housing. Our close neighbors ranged from good—Frank Komas and his daughter Susan, Bruce and Nan Shelly, Charlie and Shirley Brown—to unfortunate. Moving in, we found space in the living area for our baby grand piano, handsome secretary and nice couches. We replaced the heavy spring-balanced garage door with a quieter rollup door. We had a family room, powder room, living and dining rooms downstairs, a master bedroom, guest

136

room, office/den and two bathrooms upstairs. Once we had settled in, the place became quite comfortable.

A close neighbor was Mike Reed, who made his living producing computer software. He was about our age, a good tennis player, and a pleasant companion for afternoon "happy hour" at the common area's small swimming pool. Others were Ursula and Frank Gusdorf, a bit older than we. They came from Europe and had traveled there often: England, Germany, etc. He was an accomplished artist in pen-and-ink and in watercolor; several of his paintings are valued family possessions. We particularly like his close-up waterside views of "the Old Country."

Before leaving Los Altos we had been adopted by a stray kitten. The poor little girl came and parked on our back stoop–hungry, abused, with a collar so tight it choked her. We took her in, got her examined by a veterinarian and made her welcome. She was completely white, so Raymonde called her Edelweis, the name of a small, white flower that cloaks the Alpine hills in summertime. She became a treasure.

Taking active part in neighborhood association affairs, Ray served several years on the Hearings and Appeals Committee. Most of its business involved parking violations and careless entry of the complex (also known as "jumping the gate"). I was a consistent member of the Architectural Control Committee, and for one year I was a member of the board of directors of the association.

The association constituted a sort of political entity in miniature–elections, volunteer work, a small support staff. There was cleavage between liberals–"if someone violates a rule, commiserate with him and ask him to do better,"–and conservatives–"fine him so he will remember." Cliques of residents formed on both sides of various issues: fewer speed bumps or more, let go the gate guards or retain them, keep the current landscaping contractor or find a new one, etc. Major controversy arose over the choice of house color–dark brown garage doors and trim versus the pale beige "Los-Angeles-style." Things were kept lively and contentious.

In recreational activities, Ray and I did well in swimming and poorly in tennis. A two or three table bridge group met informally. In the Santa Clara Valley, someone had organized an Alliance Francaise for the study of French literature and practice of the language. Raymonde took part in this and enjoyed it thoroughly. Especially exciting was the Alliance's annual wine festival to celebrate "le Beaujolais Nouveau," which followed the French tradition of celebrating the release of Beaujolais wine bottled "new," directly after fermentation at the end of each harvest season.

I retired from SRI in May 1991 with the status of principal scientist. Ray reduced her part-time nursing activities to some six days a month. We were financially comfortable, having left our SRI retirement funds intact to accumulate. Also, it wasn't long before I had no more Santa Clara University courses to teach. It appeared that interest in applied mathematics had waned in the face of student concentration on computer software: graphics display, communications, and "object-oriented" code.

Thus, there was time for social activity. We renewed our acquaintance with Jane and Joe Auckenthaler, he being a son of Raymonde's Aunt Alice. He had come from Switzerland to the U.S. after the van Laars. Jane is a lovely lady and very good friend. She and Joe had met while skiing at Squaw Valley, and now lived in Hillsborough just an easy drive from Los Gatos.

A particularly enjoyable jaunt was a weekend trip to Pennsylvania. Raymonde's good friend from La Cour Plante, Kitty Belle Tibbetts, with whom she had kept contact, had married a lawyer named Tom Steiger. They lived on a farm near Mercersburg, PA raising cattle. Their home was a handsome, two-story, grey stone building of considerable age in a picturesque countryside setting. Kitty and Ray were delighted to renew their friendship and recount their memories of France. Tom was a U.S. Navy veteran of World War II with service in the Pacific; he and I could tell sea stories. It was great to visit with them.

In 1995 Matthew's duty took him to the U.S. Army War College; he, Ginny and Zachary moved to a house on a large lot in Carlisle, Pennsylvania. Sometime around August of that year, Raymonde and Ginny undertook a trip to Switzerland. Matt was away, so Zachary and I did the housekeeping; fortunately the two of us survived. We both remembered vividly the sight at Dulles Airport of Ray and Ginny embarking down the airplane loading ramp, laughing and giggling like a pair of schoolgirls just released from detention. The two ladies returned, happily recounting their visits to Lausanne, Montreux and other Swiss locations. They had had a particularly pleasant evening of dinner and conversation with the Auckenthaler cousins, whom they had not seen in several years.

Ray and I took one of our most successful business/pleasure trips to Europe in May of 2000. It included a cruise along the Rhine River, with visits to Strasbourg, France and Cologne, Germany. In Heidelberg we saw the medieval ruins (which the Germans blamed on the French). After the cruise we made a thankfully brief stop in Amsterdam, then went to Deauville, staying at the delightful Hotel Normandy. We had a comfortable, beautiful room overlooking the port of Le Havre and La Manche (the "English Channel") with processions of ships of all kinds. Horseback riders on the beach evoked happy memories for Raymonde. We rented a car and went sightseeing to Villers-sur-Mer. We were excited to see Raymonde's old school, Ecole Jean d'Arc still in operation. Furthermore, in Trouville we found her high school, Lycee Marie Joseph, operating but now admitting male students; Raymonde considered this to be a decline in quality of education. We drove to see the beaches of the 1944 Allied invasion, including the magnificent American cemetery. On a day's visit to the spectacular town-abbey-fortress, Monte St. Michel, we had lunch at La Mere Poulard's restaurant–traditional omelette, ham and white wine. We asked for lobster salad, but when the waiter presented a healthy live lobster for our approval, we took one look at it and asked, "You are going to kill it for us?" In horror, we cancelled the order. The waiter went away muttering something about "ces sacres americaines."

During our time in Los Gatos, some of our days were made memorable by visits to or from our children. A tour of duty brought Matthew to the U.S. Navy Post-Graduate School at Monterey; he, Ginny and Zachary got together with us fairly often. Carmel and Pacific Grove nearby are distinctive towns with colonial architecture, nice restaurants and tourist attractions. Young Zack could be a handful–one look into his room could bring an expression of dismay to his grandmother's face–but he was smart, strong and likeable, so it was easy for him to win her affection and regard. Charles was busy with his work, conducting missile tests at Pt. Mugu. He had bought a comfortable two-story house in Ventura. Raymonde and I could drive down there for a three-day visit. We enjoyed his company and his stories of flights of remote-controlled airplane targets. Cocktails at the roof lounge of the Ventura Holiday Inn were a treat. It became something of a habit to celebrate New Year's Eve in Los Gatos at one of several local clubs with all the family gathered happily.

New orders sent Ginny's family to Norfolk, Virginia, where Matthew took command of the USS *Normandy*, a guided-missile-armed cruiser. On a visit, Raymonde and I were invited on a dependants' day short cruise aboard his ship which took us out of Norfolk Navy Base to beyond Cape Charles, returning in the afternoon with a flyby of Navy jets. Raymonde did thoroughly enjoy sitting in the Captain's chair, watching the ship's maneuvers and basking in the Captain's hospitality.

The years go quickly and Raymonde and I soon found ourselves in our early 70s. Around this time we assessed that we had indeed reached a ripe old age and decided it was high time to put our legal affairs in order. Much of the impulse behind this step came from the fact that our own parents had not taken such measures. Charles and Dichette left no wills or final directions, so medical decisions and funeral arrangements were dropped in the hands of their children, who did not always cooperate. When my father died my mother's major asset was their home in Richmond, for which we could find no deed papers; in dealing with the resulting problems of settling their affairs we were lucky to avoid any major intra-family bitterness.

With the help of Henry W. Roux, a Los Gatos lawyer, Raymonde and I updated our trust agreement. Also, we made and filed wills, durable powers of attorney for assets, and advanced health care directives.

Thus it was that we settled into a comfortable, old-married-couple mode of living. We both kept ourselves in fairly good shape, Ray at 113 lbs, me at 158. Our division of labor had Raymonde keeping the bank accounts and spending the money, me doing household fix-up work and tinkering with sailing ship models. Afternoon "happy hours" on a back patio, often with Frank Komas, were most pleasant.

There were occasional differences of opinion that could become emphatic. For example, when it came time to buy a new automobile, Ray never saw the virtues of sports-car styling and "four-on-the-floor." We had learned how to work such things out, even if the process did sometimes include a day of silent treatment. Between us there was remembered physical ecstasy, great affection, mutual respect and very real love.

On a quiet, autumn afternoon in late 2005, Raymonde suffered a stroke. She and I were relaxing and enjoying some wine on our patio when it happened. I saw the convulsion of muscles in her face, her stricken expression, her sudden inability to hold her glass. I took her to El Camino Hospital emergency room, and there found in attendance (by great good fortune) Dr.

Steven Carlson, one of our favorite physicians. He put her in the hospital for two days. She came out with her left arm and leg disabled. At home she did fairly well, until one afternoon, on her way downstairs, she had a bad fall. A small fracture in her shoulder led to a week's recuperation and then to physical therapy, which she hated–"They are trying to break my bones again!"

Her injuries made home life difficult. At the end of some days, she complained of such pain that we took her back to the hospital where X-rays showed a fractured spinal disc. The prescription for care was simply rest in bed and pain medication. She was taken to a skilled nursing facility, which she also hated. After two weeks, we decided with the approval of her primary care physician, Dr. Alison Dowes–a great lady–to undertake a regime of home care.

Patient care in a two-story home like ours in Rinconada Hills requires considerable organization. Ginny and Chuck came at various times to supervise/ outfit/assist. We installed powered chair lifts on the stairs. We built a ramp for the master bathroom shower and acquired a shower chair, a wheelchair and bed-care equipment. Services four hours a day, five days a week by a nurse-aide were procured from Geriatric Home Care Specialists. The ladies who came on this job were all efficient, companionable and sympathetic. They provided assistance with showers and cleaning; help with wheelchair activities; patient care when I had to run an errand; and assistance with the fairly complicated operation of getting Raymonde to the dentist. I took responsibility for administering prescription medication, preparing meals and providing companionship and affection. It was a happy distraction when nephew Douglas Foy brought his family for an afternoon's visit and his sweet, lovely wife Nancy sat with Raymonde in her bedroom.

It is said that nurses and doctors make bad patients, and Raymonde was not an exception. In general, she wanted little more than rest in bed and relief from pain. The children and I had hoped that with time and care, her back injury would heal. Then she could take an interest in reading, music and some physical activity (the television in her room stayed off most of the time). What's more, we planned on getting her outside and in the car for a nice ride once in a while.

All such exertion Raymonde resisted. Indeed it involved more pain when we tried it than she was willing to tolerate. A trip downstairs and out to the car brought strong complaints. Just to sit up in the wheelchair was more than she wanted to do for very long. And she knew how to make her objections forceful. I always remembered how, on a regular trip via chair to the bathroom shower, Raymonde remarked emphatically, "This is no way to treat a lady!"

Dr. Dowes came to visit and check on her patient. The visiting nurse from the care provider came every other week. In this way, Raymonde's home care regime continued for about a year. It involved progressively stronger medication for pain relief and it meant a slow deterioration in health. On the evening of 3 December 2006, with me on my bed beside her, Raymonde went peacefully to sleep and, during the night, slipped quietly away from this life.

8

✤

LOVE ALWAYS, DEAREST, WADE

The most explicit and concise philosophy of life I know is the motto of the U.S. Military Academy at West Point, New York: Duty, Honor, Country.

For Raymonde, the two countries of her allegiance were Switzerland and the United States of America. The former, because she was born and raised there, and because the relatives she most admired, and with whom she felt most comfortable lived there. The landscape of Switzerland is beautiful, despite the efforts of graffiti splashers to deface it. Certainly the view of a mountain like the Jungfrau, snow-covered all year long, will inspire most anyone. It was at the tuberculosis clinic in Leysin, canton of Vaud, that Ray carried out her best and most successful nursing work. For travel or vacation she always preferred to visit Switzerland, and she followed political developments and financial crises there with close attention. Over the course of her life, Raymonde's homeland dealt with major policy issues—participation in the European Common Market and later in the European Union, the right of women to vote—and Raymonde had strong opinions on all of these, heavily influenced by her firm belief in Swiss nationality.

Her entry into the U.S. was not graced by much of

a welcome. There was bureaucratic monkey business about changing her passport from Dutch to Swiss so that she could come in as an immigrant. The failure of U.S. institutions to recognize her French and Swiss nursing experience, and her inability at first to find a job better than lower tier, were major disappointments. But she persevered and, with the help of night schools and her own courage, earned higher quality work. When she finally, after more bureaucratic turmoil and passing-around of papers, earned her U.S. citizenship, it was a great day of pride and happiness.

With her feet firmly planted on U.S. soil, she took her citizen duties seriously and carried them out actively. She exercised her right to vote at every opportunity, and she made a conscientious effort to understand the issues and candidates. This led her to active work in Republican Party affairs; her conservative philosophy of government strengthened through these experiences. It happened—not by accident—that these beliefs were passed along intact to our children.

A sense of duty was important to Raymonde. Her work as an X-ray technologist was done carefully, efficiently and accurately; it often won the praise of her supervisors and Radiologists. When she was on nursing staff, she was punctual, knowledgeable and especially careful with prescription medication. She never joined a labor union (partly because a lot of her work was part-time), which sometimes led to arguments with some colleagues. A constant characteristic was the sympathy and understanding she showed to her patients.

In carrying out her duties as a mother she believed in close attention, much love and discipline modified by humor and affection. She raised our children and nurtured them carefully. I know that our son Charles, as an adult, retained his admiration and respect for his mother. I have heard our daughter Ginny tell how, when faced with some problem, she would ask herself, "How would Mom do this?" Their mother could be both a goad and a guide. Further, she could be generous, both with her time and with financial or material aid. Everyone in our family benefited from the advice or help that she gave willingly.

Raymonde cultivated in her husband and children an appreciation of fine things. One of her favorite movies was "The Prisoner of Zenda" with Ronald Coleman and Madeleine Carroll. In art she most admired the work of Cezanne and Renoir. The paintings and watercolors she bought were seascapes and European scenes by local or little-known artists, chosen for their personal appeal. Opera did not go over well, though. On a trip to Vienna we actually, with excellent seats, walked away at intermission from a performance of Mozart's "The Magic Flute"–the music was great, but everything else was a sad mish-mash. Raymonde's favorite music was that of List, Chopin and Beethoven. The first records we bought, when newly married and settled, were Tchaikovsky's "Capriccio Italienne" and Bizet's "Symphony in C." To maintain her practice of French she subscribed to the Cercle du Livre de France; she particularly enjoyed it when an author made beautiful use of the language. Fine china was a strong interest. Ray had a special liking for small, individually decorated demi-tasse cups and saucers. She assembled an excellent collection, and was particularly pleased when she found a Limoge item. As you might expect, her tastes were definitely in the classical domain.

Nowhere do I intend to imply that my wife was a candidate for sainthood. She had a strong personality and clung fast to her principles. At times when I would tell her on some subject that compromise was in order, she would tell me to stop being "wishy-washy"–along with other things. Learning English in New York City night class, she picked up a lot of not-quite-lady-like U.S. slang. Raymonde was something of a "good hater." When a person or idea made it into her black book, it could take a long time for them to get back in her good graces, and sometimes they never did. She was consistent in her beliefs and approvals. I was very fortunate in that she loved me dearly.

Even in our times of being "poor like rats," Raymonde practiced her own style of good dress and deportment. In the best sense of the phrase, she was a lady with class.

This brings me to consider her sense of honor. Raymonde and I shared a strong regard for our marriage vows, and recognized our obligations under them. We were faithful to each other from the day we met. Indeed, we were deeply in love for fifty-five years. Of all the ways to describe this state, I know of no better words than those of Robert Burns:

"O my luve is like a red, red rose,
That's newly sprung in June:
O my luve is like the melodie,
That's sweetly play'd in tune.

As fair art thou, my bonnie lass,
So deep in luve am I;
And I will luve thee still, my dear,
Till a' the seas gang dry."

www.ingramcontent.com/pod-product-compliance
Lightning Source LLC
Chambersburg PA
CBHW030941150426
42812CB00064B/3088/J